KEEPING VISITORS

A Systematic Approach to
Assimilate Visitors into Your Church

Gil Stieglitz

KEEPING VISITORS

© Gil Stieglitz 2016

Published by Principles to Live By, Roseville CA 95661
www.ptlb.com

Cover Design by John Chase
Copyediting by Jennifer Edwards
Book Design by Linné Garrett

All Rights Reserved. No part of this publication may be reproduced, stored in a retrieval system, or transmitted in any way by any means –electronic, mechanical, photocopy, recording, or otherwise – without the prior permission of the copyright holder, except as provided by USA copyright law.

All Scripture verses are from the New American Standard
Bible unless otherwise indicated.
New American Standard Bible: 1995 update.
1995 La Habra, CA: The Lockman Foundation.

ISBN 978-0-9968855-0-8
Christian Living

Printed in the United States of America

This Book is Dedicated To:

Dr. Conrad Lowe, Dr. John Maxwell, and Dr. Gary McIntosh, who have all taught me so much about how to lead, grow, and develop the Community of Faith that we call the church. I owe each of these men a great debt for the wisdom they have imparted to me over the years.

Table of Contents

Introduction to the L.E.A.D.E.R.S.H.O.P. System 7

Introduction to Keeping Visitors 17

Chapter 1: Community Awareness Strategy 27

Chapter 2: First Visit Strategy. 59

Chapter 3: First Weeks Strategy 79

Chapter 4: First Year Strategy 101

Chapter 5: Church Orientation Strategy 111

Chapter 6: Small Group Life Strategy 119

Chapter 7: Service Strategy 127

Chapter 8: Friendship Strategy 159

Conclusion 183

How to Use This Book Effectively 193

About the Author. 195

Other Resources. 196

Introduction to The L.E.A.D.E.R.S.H.O.P. System

It is often hard for the leaders of a church to see how their own church is mired in a systemic problem. Many times it's easier to blame people and particular incidents that have supposedly crippled the church, rather than to take a deeper look. When we look at the church as a creation that God designed to take sinners and turn them into saints, we can see where things are working and where breakdowns occur.

The sinner-to-saint process requires certain systems to be put in place and intentionality within those systems. If there are breakdowns in those systems, then the church will get stuck as it strives to achieve its maximum potential.

The book you are holding in your hand is one part of a whole system for understanding and strengthening the local church. It is called The L.E.A.D.E.R.S.H.O.P. System. Each letter stands for one of the ten major systems that must operate smoothly for a ministry to be healthy.

L stands for the **Leadership System**, which controls the direction, management, and ability of the organization to train up new leaders.

E stands for the **Evangelism System**, which determines how many people can connect to the Lord Jesus through the ministries of the church.

A stands for the **Assimilation System**, which determines how many people can connect to and remain in the local church.

D stands for the **Discipleship System**, which controls the maturity of those who are in the church.

E stands for the **Equipping System**, which controls who, how well, and how many can be put into service for the Lord, both in and out of the church.

R stands for the **Resources System**, which controls the amount of funds and facilities that the church collects, erects, and uses to accomplish its mission.

S stands for the **Spiritual System,** which controls how spiritually active the people in the church are in both a corporate and individual sense.

H stands for the **Heart System,** which controls the amount of love, care, and compassion that exists within and flows out of the church.

O stands for the **Organizational System,** which helps people understand the ways that the organization of the church must change as the church gets larger, and how staff fits into that organization.

P stands for the **Purpose System,** which directs the accomplishment of the purpose of the church in every aspect of ministry.

This series of books, tapes, and videos are designed to give pastors, lay leaders, and general Christians, practical tools to diagnose, repair, and improve the various systems in their church, so that their church can be maximally effective for the glory of the Lord.

The L.E.A.D.E.R.S.H.O.P. System
Church Health Survey

There are ten systems operating in every ministry. The health of those systems determines the health of the whole ministry. This survey will identify a ministry's *top two systems* and *bottom two systems*. A focus on the bottom two systems for a year will usually result in the greatest change in the health of the ministry. To maximize the validity of the survey, have at least twenty-five people in the ministry take the survey.

SCORE:
1 = never | 3 = occasionally | 5 = sometimes
8 = usually | 10 = always

_____ This ministry is healthy and vibrant.

_____ This ministry has compelling specific goals for the next few years and mobilizes people to accomplish them.

_____ This ministry leads people to faith in Christ.

_____ Each major event is promoted at least seven different ways.

_____ This ministry changes people's lives.

_____ This ministry regularly recruits and deploys new people into serving in the church.

THE L.E.A.D.E.R.S.H.O.P SYSTEM CHURCH HEALTH SURVEY

_____ This ministry spends money on life transformation, new converts, and tangible help to the poor, deep connection between Christians, and increasing God's reputation and glory.

_____ The worship services of this ministry consistently enrapture people into God's presence and exalt His name.

_____ People in this ministry are filled up emotionally, spiritually, relationally, and mentally by their involvement.

_____ This ministry has a system, person, or program already in place to deal with the majority of the needs that arise in ministry.

_____ The average person could state the five reasons for the church.

_____ This ministry builds up at least six to ten new godly leaders every year.

_____ Evangelism is a high priority in this ministry.

_____ On a person's first visit, they are welcomed and made to feel comfortable by at least six different people in various parts of the facility.

_____ This ministry produces a mature Christian after a certain period of time — a transformed person after long-term exposure to the ministry.

_____ This ministry trains people to do ministry effectively.

_____ This ministry has people that regularly give tithes and offerings to help advance the life-transformational ministries of the church.

INTRODUCTIONS

_____ This ministry shows people how to draw near to God each week.

_____ The community knows that God loves them through this ministry.

_____ This ministry uses part-time directors and lay leaders to head up significant ministry areas.

_____ The ministry leaders pray and plan the ministry's specific goals and not uninvolved oversight committees.

_____ People know what the specific goals are for the next twelve months.

_____ This ministry uses a variety of ways to present the gospel.

_____ The church warmly contacts the visitor at least six different times in the first two weeks.

_____ Every week the instruction in this ministry causes people to apply the Bible to their lives.

_____ This ministry helps people uncover their "gifted" ministry place.

_____ This ministry uses its present facilities wisely.

_____ This ministry is very effective at praying and seeing God answer.

_____ People develop deep friendships in this ministry.

THE L.E.A.D.E.R.S.H.O.P SYSTEM CHURCH HEALTH SURVEY

____ The ministry staff are initiating leaders and thrusting their ministry forward and into new areas.

____ The programs and sub-ministries actually accomplish the purposes of the ministry.

____ Pastors and leaders read books, listen to tapes, and attend conferences to keep learning.

____ This ministry trains its members on how to witness effectively.

____ In their first year, a visitor has been invited to the pastor's home, become a part of a small group, attended some classes on how the church and Christianity works, has three new friends, and serves the church in some way.

____ People in this ministry practice their faith during the week.

____ The leaders of this ministry delegate whole sections of ministry to people they have raised up.

____ This ministry plans ahead for future facility needs.

____ God's blessing and presence is all over this ministry.

____ This ministry cares for the unlovely, afflicted, oppressed, and poor.

____ The decision-making process in this church is effective and known.

____ This ministry is innovative but not gimmicky or fad-driven.

Understanding Your Ministry Score

There are ten systems operating in every ministry, and the health of each system is critical for the health of the whole ministry. There were four questions given for each of the systems. The score for each system can be determined by adding up the questions from each system. You are looking to identify your *two strongest systems* and your *two weakest systems*. You will be tempted to try and work on all of the systems at once; this is unwise and usually results in little, if any, progress.

Instead, identify your two weakest systems and focus attention, resources, and change in these two areas and the ministry will see the greatest improvement. Note what you are doing that makes your strongest systems strong and keep doing those actions. They will automatically improve just by realizing what you are doing well.

As the church pushes through each new size barrier, the survey results will change and the systems will need to be re-evaluated for the new size. Take your scores from the survey and total them for your system score.

The Ten
L.E.A.D.E.R.S.H.O.P. Systems
Health Assessment Scoring

Leadership System: Q. 2, 12, 22, 32

Evangelism System: Q. 3, 13, 23, 33

Assimilation System: Q. 4, 14, 24, 34

Discipleship System: Q. 5, 15, 25, 35

Equipping System: Q. 6, 16, 26, 36

Resources System: Q. 7, 17, 27, 37

Spiritual System: Q. 8, 18, 28, 38

Heart System: Q. 9, 19, 29, 39

Organization System: Q. 10, 20, 30, 40

Purpose System: Q. 11, 21, 31, 41

Overview of the whole ministry: All

INTRODUCTIONS

Introduction to Keeping Visitors

Most pastors and church leaders ask questions like:
How can I keep more of the visitors who come to the church?
Why don't we hang on to the people who visit our church?
How can I assimilate the people who come to the church?
How can I close the back door of the church?

As the pastor of my church, I had the same kind of questions. We decided to develop a strategy to see what we could do to hold on to the people who entered our doors and assimilate them into the ministry. When we began implementing this system, our retention rate of visitors went from 23% to 82%.

Other churches using this system within their settings are also reporting huge jumps in retention of visitors. One even went as high as attaining a 93% retention rate! Most pastors and lay leaders are doing the best they can and only need some new ideas and a more comprehensive picture.

This book is designed to help churches and ministries increase visitor retention with a practical and workable system.

Assimilation System Implementation
Increasing Retention Rates of Visitors

Early one summer a number of years ago, I was enjoying being a pastor. Everything was going well in the church. We were assimilating about 23% of the people who came to visit and we had a healthy, thriving, and expanding congregation. But disaster struck. The major industry supporting our town was severely downsized. A steady stream of people in the church came to see me to tell me that they had to move because they were losing their house. They had been laid off. Three quarters of the homes in our town eventually were boarded up as people lost jobs, homes, cars, everything. It was an absolute nightmare. Our church lost 119 tithing families in a three-month period. We were saying good-bye to longstanding members every week. It was tragic! Our church started to shrink quickly, and we were in trouble.

Fortunately, there were new families visiting the church, but with a 23% retention rate, we could not stop shrinking. We had to act fast. This crisis necessitated a total revamp of our strategy for getting people *attracted* and *attached* to our congregation. We had to become experts at welcoming new people into our church or we would quickly cease to exist. We began to embrace a whole different way of approaching each and every visitor that attended our church.

We set out to be intentionally interested in our visitors for a whole year to give them every opportunity to find Christ and make our church their church home.

We began doing a number of things we had never done before. Because we were intentional in implementing our assimilation strategies, our church went from 23% to 82% assimilation of visitors. We stopped shrinking, and we even started growing again. Yes, it was a great deal of work to focus on welcoming and assimilating visitors, but it was well worth it. If we had not made those changes, our church would have shrunk to almost non-existence.

We discovered we had been relying on the visitors themselves to keep wanting to connect with us until they were a part of the church. In this day and age, that isn't a reliable strategy, especially for non-Christians, as the church is not the driving force of their lives yet. Many churches are made up of people who have been around church all their lives, and they just internally know how to make connections with a church. Most visitors are not like this. They do not know the inner workings of a church and probably don't know anyone at the church. They may even have suspicions about church in general based on past experiences or preconceived notions. Visitors often see the church as a business that will guide them to a relationship with God and/or others of a like mind. The visitor's mindset and assumption is that the church will do the work of connecting them to others and to God. This requires that the church think through the steps of welcoming and assimilating visitors into the church.

Many churches have not done adequate planning and team building to accomplish this task of connecting visitors into informed, close friendships with others at the church. When our church took the time to actually think through how we could help the visitor make a solid connection with the church, our visitor retention rate went way up. When a church plans, anticipates, and strategizes how to make connections to the church easier, it becomes significantly easier for the visitor to continue going to the church.

Life Development Plan

It is very important to understand that the *Assimilation System* is only a small part of an overall *Life Development Plan* geared toward attracting and attaching visitors to your church. Each church should have a *Life Development Plan* for individuals that come to the church, which includes a number of steps in a person's spiritual journey to become a fully devoted follower of Jesus Christ. It is the church's mission to have a clear understanding of each major step in that spiritual journey and how to move a person from where they are to the next step in the journey. The goal of the church is to work with, on, and for the people who are connected and connecting to the church until we all obtain to the full maturity of the knowledge of Jesus Christ (Eph. 4:11-13).

We are not just trying to get people to attend our church so that our church is bigger. We are trying to move people to become fully devoted followers of Christ. We want everyone to finish the spiritual journey of becoming an ambassador for Christ. At each stage, an individual has the potential to stagnate and stop moving forward in maturity. We need to be able to identify where people fall through the cracks and where they tend to stagnate.

Seven Stages of Spiritual Maturity

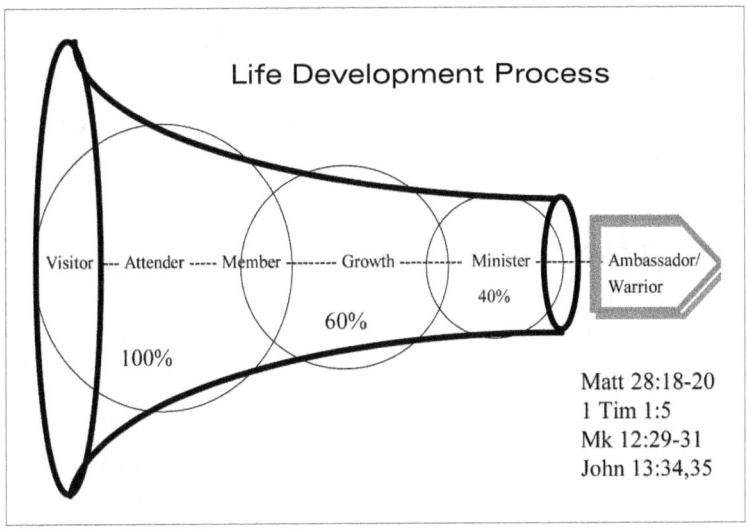

Stage 1: Community Member
This is the person, who lives within the region that the church serves, but does not attend the church.

Stage 2: Visitor
This is the person, who visits the church for the first time or even occasionally comes, but is not a regular.

Stage 3: Attender
This is the person who regularly comes but has not committed to becoming a Christian or a member of the church.

Stage 4: Member
This is the person who has joined the church.

Stage 5: Maturing
This is the person, who continues to mature in their Christian life.

Stage 6: Active Servant
This is the person, who is discovering how to serve the church in the most effective way.

Stage 7: Agent of God
This is the person whose faith is active during the week beyond Sunday morning.

These seven stages are significant in the development of a person into a fully matured Christian. Most people drop out of involvement with church and God between one of these stages. They may set out to get to the next stage, but they do not make it all the way to the next place.

Between each of these stages of development, it is possible for them to fall through the cracks and not be involved, and/or to stagnate and stop making progress. Some people think about coming to church but never make it. Some people visit the church once but do not make it back for a variety of reasons, or do not connect to the church. Some people attend regularly, but they never become Christians or members of the church; they just attend. Some people become members but don't grow up in their Christian faith; they stagnate at the commitment level of a member without the progress into maturity. Some people grow in their maturity in Christ, but they do not become fully active in service for the Lord; they just never find their God-directed areas of most effective service. Some people are active servants for the Lord in church but never take their faith to the marketplace or into their neighborhood; they have stagnated in the church.

There is a significant commitment required to move from one of these stages to the next. Progress between any of these stages is good but requires desire and effort. The church can encourage and promote the movement between the various stages of the spiritual growth through prayer, planning, strategy, hard work, and a compelling presentation of Christian information, teamwork, and love.

We are really asking what must be done to, with, on, and for the individual to help them make the next step in their spiritual journey. How do we draw them or motivate them to visit the church? How do we get them to bridge the gap between visitor and attender? What can the people of the church do to cause and strengthen the attender to take the next step and become a member?

The church cannot make a person move from one stage of spiritual development to the next, but they can strategically think about removing barriers to progress their spiritual development forward. They can also design into the church's interaction with people things that will motivate the person to take the next step in spiritual development.

Asking these kinds of questions is often a completely different way of examining the church's mission and role in an individual's life — especially the visitor's. To actually plan out the typical elements that a person needs in order to move forward in the initial steps of connection with a church is ignored as too simplistic or even manipulative. But to see this level of planning as important to spiritual development of every person who comes to the church brings a whole new perspective to the assimilation process.

Many churches cannot grow even if they assimilate new people because they are up against a size barrier. Many churches stagnate in weekly attendance around predictable numbers: 40-50, 80-100, 160-200, 400-500, 800-1,000, 1,600-2,000, 3,200-5,000, etc. These size barriers are really organizational barriers that require a church to be organized differently in order to continue growing. There is not the time to fully develop this idea in this introduction, but I have watched many pastors focus exclusively on the assimilation system in their church and have no rise in attendance because the problem is one of organization and size and not assimilation. In these cases, if the pastor were to focus on organizing the church for the next size and implement an effective assimilation system, then growth would follow — often dramatically.

Four Key Assimilation Strategies

The assimilation process that we are going to explain to you really does work. It is not personality-driven but reaches out with the love of Christ and welcomes people into a community of faith. In order to attract and attach visitors to your church and to God, there are four separate overarching strategies that need to be implemented, all of which need to work together smoothly. These four strategies could be called a *Visitor Flow System*, or *Assimilation System*.

Keeping in mind the comprehensive nature of *"KEEPING VISITORS,"* you can see from the chart below at what stages the *Assimilation System* can be implemented to move people from awareness of your church, to visiting, to membership, and to maturity. It is imperative to grasp the comprehensive nature of these four strategies and how they overlap so we can keep the visitor from dropping out of church life before they have been connected to people, God, and the mission of the church.

Grasping the overview is important, otherwise it's easy to get lost in the details and lose sight of the overarching pillars of the whole system. There will be many details for each aspect of the system. The larger the church, the more details you will need to use to fill out that specific part of the overall system. But you must begin with understanding the overview of the basic steps that will take a visitor and connect them to the people of your church over a year.

All four strategies are listed in the chart below, which gives a good overview of the system. We'll then look at each strategy in depth.

The Assimilation System

STRATEGY	EXPLANATION
Community Awareness	This is the church's way of drawing individuals and families into the church. If there is no visitor, there will be no assimilation.
1st Visit	This is the church's plan for what it will do for a visitor on their first Sunday so that the visitor will want to come back the next week and in the weeks to come.
1st Weeks	This is the church's plan for what it will do for a visitor between the first Sunday the visitor comes and the next few Sundays so that the visitor wants to come back. This is where they will have most of their questions answered.
1st Year	This is the church's plan for what it will do for the visitor after the first few weeks so that the visitor will continue to come, will become a Christian, and will be incorporated into the life of the church.

Chapter 1

Community Awareness Strategy

Every church needs to think through their response to Jesus' repeated commands to proclaim the gospel to every person. How often do you try and impact the community with the message of your church? How much are you willing to spend to let the community know that the church is open for business? How is your church going to compel the people in the community around your church to visit your church for the first time? What kinds of methods are you going to use to let people know that they should visit your church? Do the people in the region around your church know what your church is like? Do they have a positive or negative impression about your church? Do they have any impression about your church? Actually, every church has a Community Awareness Philosophy that is already delivering the number of visitors that are currently coming to the church; the reality of how many visitors are coming is evidence of that philosophy.

There are several key assumptions that need to be factored in when developing the Community Awareness Strategy.

Assumption #1:
It takes seven impressions.

We live in an advertising-saturated society in North America. Thousands of messages bombard everyone each day. In many ways, we have learned to tune these messages out. For this reason, it takes six to seven times of hearing or seeing an advertising message that we are interested in before we can really distinguish which store or brand is offering that product. So in order for your church to break through the natural defensiveness of people, they will have to hear about your church from lots of different places in lots of different ways.

Assumption #2:
Eighty percent+ of your community does not notice your church or know what you do in there.

Some pastors and lay leaders have the idea that just because they know about the church and think about it all the time that everyone else knows about the church and that they should come. This is just not true. Many people rarely think about the church, and when they do, they do not think about your church. Many people do not connect their problems and possible solutions with church. Most people in our world today do not think that they are estranged from God and are in need of a Savior who can put them back in right relationship with God. This is the reason they are not beating down the doors to our churches hoping that we have room for them. We must engage them in some fashion to get them to want to come to the church and check out the community of faith to learn about Jesus.

In most communities in the United States, until your church is 400+ in size, the people in the community do not even notice that your church is there. In some communities the number is 1,000+. This is difficult for the average pastor to believe, but it is absolutely true. I was doing some consulting work for a friend of mine in a city in the southwestern United States. At the time, this town had only two protestant churches over one hundred in Sunday morning attendance. My friend's church was one of those churches. He had done a wonderful job of growing this church from twenty to over 125 people attending. He is a very diligent pastor and evangelist. But since his church was under four hundred, I told him and his people that the church was probably unknown in the city. My friend didn't believe me, especially since he witnessed to everyone and talked about his church.

We were out at the Dairy Queen for lunch one day, and my friend was carrying on a conversation with the young lady behind the counter. She obviously knew my friend and knew that he was a pastor. He had invited her to church on numerous occasions. Just to prove my point, when I got to the counter, I asked the young lady if she knew my friend. She said she did. I asked her if she knew that he was a pastor. She said that she did. I asked her where his church was located. She thought for a moment and said that she did not know. My friend, who was standing there, was dumbstruck. He couldn't believe it. He asked her, "You don't know where my church is?" She sheepishly said, "No." He pointed over her shoulder through the drive-through window to the building at the end of the street, "That is my church!" "Oh," is all she said. Most people do not notice a church building they do not attend until it is over four hundred in size and has lots of programs and activities that get it noticed.

We have to realize that one of our jobs is to let people know we are open for business. We are in the saving business and everyone in the community ought to know it. Jesus said to shout it from the rooftops! You have to make them aware of the good that will come to them if they attend your church.

We live in an advertising-saturated society in which people are bombarded by groups and organizations wanting their attention. If you do not have a workable, consistent strategy that will help the gospel and your individual church break through the fog of all the messages that people hear, you will be invisible to the people in the community that you want to come to your church. Let me say that in a slightly different way. Right now, you are invisible to many, if not most, of the people in your community who need to come to your church. The church has the benefit that no ordinary advertiser has in that God the Holy Spirit draws people to the Lord Jesus for salvation. It would, however, be foolish to ignore what God has told us to do and put the burden on Him completely. We need to publish the good news. We need to do everything we can to compel them to come in. We need to go out and invite everyone to come into the wedding feast of the Lamb.

Assumption #3:
If you don't have visitors, there will be no one to assimilate. You must increase visitor flow to grow.

One of the crucial questions that your church must ask and answer is: "How many people do you want to add to the church this year?" Whatever the number of people that you are praying for requires visitors. Without visitors coming to the church, nothing happens in terms of growth. To grow, you must have enough visitors to multiply by your assimilation rate. Your growth rate is:

$$\text{Visitors} \times \text{Assimilation Rate} = \text{Growth}$$

Think this through: If your church wanted to add fifty people this year to your average weekly attendance, this would mean that approximately twenty families would be attending that are not attending now. In order to gain those twenty families this year, your church must have over two hundred people visit the church this year if you have a current assimilation rate of ten percent. Obviously you want to have a better assimilation rate, but you must first answer the question of how you are going to get two hundred people to visit the church that aren't connected to the church right now. How are you going to make the community aware of the wonder and excitement that is taking place at your church so that two hundred people will come this year? Two hundred visitors in one year means that an average of four visitors a week. If you currently have less than this, then this first step of an assimilation strategy is critical for you. You have to increase visitor flow.

Too often churches just allow the visitor flow to take care of itself and want to take care of assimilating the visitors they already have coming. This neglects the fact that there are many wonderful lost people who would visit the church and come to faith in Christ if they just had a chance to hear about your church. This chapter will help you focus on creative ways to increase the visitor flow towards your church.

Assumption #4:
Six to ten percent of members will leave for various reasons every year.

Every church has to plan on the fact that 6-10% of the people, who are members or are attending the church this year, will not be attending next year. That means that if one hundred people are coming this year, six to ten of those people will not be attending next year.

People will leave because of a move. Some people will die. Some people will leave your church because they have found one they like better down the street. All of these kinds of moves will take place whether we want them to or not. Many small church pastors make a huge deal over the fact that the Smith's, the Jones', the Wright's have left the church; but this will happen every year. You must expect it and plan for the fact that this kind of turnover will take place. If the turnover is higher than 6-10%, then you might have a problem that is beyond the norm, and this may need exploration.

This turnover rate means that you must grow by six to ten people every year just to stay the same size. When I talk with pastors of churches with fewer than two hundred people, they will often talk about how excited they are because a few wonderful new couples have joined the church. They will usually name them with a real excitement in their voice. Most pastors internally believe that new couples means growth. It doesn't mean growth unless there are more new people coming than regulars leaving. If the number of new people joining is not above the

6-10% figure, then there is no real growth. Oftentimes, the same numbers of people have disengaged from the church than have been added. If new couples are added every year but the church does not grow in overall size, then the church needs to have a much higher visitor flow and/or assimilate people at a much higher rate.

> 100 visitors x 16% assimilation rate
> = 16 people added to the church

Assumption #5:
The more your community hears about your church, the more people will have the opportunity to engage and hear the gospel.

The leadership of the church must ask and answer the questions, "How does the church actually attract more people to visit each year?" "What will cause our people to invite their friends to this church?" I have talked with pastors and lay leaders in churches across the country and they often have the mistaken idea that what worked last year will bring more people this year. What you did last year attracted the number of people that it could attract. If that was enough people, then do what you did last year. But if it didn't attract the number needed to grow, then do something different or in addition to what was done the previous year.

The other mistaken idea many churches have is that if they teach a new series of messages, it will significantly change the number of visitors to the church. This will only be true if you let more people know about your messages or your church. However, different messages will only reach a certain percentage of the people.

The following seven ways are strategies to employ that can increase the outreach potential of the church. They are:

- Personal invitation
- Special events
- Mass media
- Website
- Signage
- Newsletters
- Buildings, grounds, parking

A church does not have to do all of the things listed, but adding a new way of reaching out or considering a visitor's point-of-view when it comes to these things can be significantly beneficial. A church must come to realize that each way they make the community aware that they are open for business is more people who will hear the gospel. It allows more people the opportunity to embrace the gospel message—they do not have to follow the path of self-atonement for their lives. They can accept the work of God on their behalf, a substitutionary atonement. God is willing to accept them into His forever family because of what Christ has done.

You will need to decide how many of these different ways your church will use to make the community aware that Jesus still saves and that you are a local outlet for the wonder of salvation and community.

Seven Strategies to Increase Outreach Potential of Your Church

1. Personal Invitation of FRANS

The number one way that people visit the church is through personal invitation. Someone they know invites them to come to a service at their church. This has been the number one way that people begin connecting to a church since Jesus began the church. Some statistics suggest that up to 86% of the people who visit a church for the first time come this way. Therefore, this needs to become a primary way that all people are encouraged to participate in the growth of the church. The people that your congregation will invite to your church are called FRANS. This stands for **Friends, Relatives, Associates, and Neighbors**.

These four kinds of people are the major fishing pool for who will come to the church in the future. If your church is to grow, it will grow by the invitation of the friends, relatives, associates, and neighbors of the people you already have coming. A growing church is full of people like the people you already have coming. The people that you presently have coming are the greatest fans of your church. They are repeatedly coming and encouraged enough by some aspect of the ministry of the church. You need to ask the question: "What would cause these people to overcome their normal reticence and invite people they know to a service at this church?"

What does it mean if the pastor or lay leaders ask people to bring their friends to church, but they do not invite anyone or bring anyone? This means something is wrong. Something in the services is not compelling enough for them to invite their FRANS. Too many pastors are unwilling to accept the fact that the ministries and services of the church are not compelling enough for people to invite their FRANS, but if this were not true, they would invite them. A congregation's reluctance to invite their FRANS is not because they are stubborn, disobedient, or friendless. It is because there is not a compelling reason to invite them.

We all tell our friends about good movies we have seen. We tell them about books and TV shows that we thought were good. We may even take them to a play or restaurant that we especially liked. We do this all the time. Therefore, if no one is excited enough about church to invite or bring someone, then something needs to be changed. It could be the music. It could be the sermon. It could be the people. It could be the location. It could be the style. It could be the time or length. It is something.

Let me tell you a couple of stories that illustrate this point. A friend of mine attended a church that was of a particular denomination. This friend hired some contractors out of his church to do some work at his house. While they were working at this house, the two guys asked my friend if they knew of any good churches in the area that they could invite their boss to attend. My friend looked rather puzzled because they all attended the same church. They caught the questioning stare. They exclaimed, "We know what you are thinking, 'Why don't you invite him to our church?'

Our church is okay for all of us who know everybody and the way things are done. But, this is our boss. We want him to get saved." Wow!

I can remember my own situation when I was in college.
I was attending a little church and helping out with the youth ministry, witnessing to some other teens and college kids from the neighborhood around the college that I attended. When it came time to invite them to church, I took a few weeks off from the little church I had been attending and took them to the larger church, where a famous pastor was preaching.
I did this not because I did not love the people at the small church. I did this because I wanted these people to find the Lord. I thought that they would have a better chance of finding the Lord if they were introduced to a church that had a higher level of excellence and fit their culture better.

What will your church do to increase the number of people who invite their FRANS?

2. Special On-Site Events

Forty percent of new people's first contact with a church is by attending a big event at the church facilities. Hosting special events is one way to make it easier for people to invite their FRANS. Churches that have a high number of visitors have special events that many people would be interested in attending. Events provide an easy way to bring up reasons for coming to the church, especially when the church provides business cards, printed invitations, hand-outs, door hangers, and mail-out flyers that the congregation can give away to people at their work and their social networks. These things communicate the special things going on at the church. The materials should be good quality and consistent with the look and feel of your church brand. We found that handing out very nice, high quality personal invitations to folks in the church that they could take and hand to others was a huge hit. They could take as many invitations as they thought they could pass out. Everyone in the church could feel proud to hand out this kind of invitation to a FRANS.

There are two different kinds of special events that allow the people of the church to invite their friends to the church. There are Sunday morning special events, in which special worship elements are added to the Sunday morning worship service to encourage people to invite their FRANS to the church service. And there are special events that are held at the church, which are not particularly religious in nature. Both kinds of these "special" events are helpful in allowing people to visit the church and encourage the people of the church to invite their FRANS.

Sunday Morning Special Events

For a long time, church leaders have found that the easiest way to assimilate people into the life of the church is to have them enjoy the Sunday morning worship service. The effective visitor flow service needs to be a great service that shows off the strengths of your church. It should not be so dissimilar to your normal church service that people know that next week will be nothing like the week they came.

Many churches have found that if they schedule a special singer, drama team, a special, interesting sermon topic, or children's number as a part of the worship service, people are more willing to invite their FRANS to the service. This has caused a number of churches to include these kinds of elements in their worship service once a month, or even every week.

The ideas are nearly endless when it comes to these kinds of elements that encourage people to invite their friends to morning services: baptisms, awards ceremonies, children's drama, out-of-town choirs or musical groups, drama groups, special singers, baby dedications, community recognitions, special speakers, special sermon topics, etc. Pastors and lay leaders often find that certain kinds of worship elements encourage people to invite their FRANS more than other events. As long as the elements that are added to the worship service are truly magnifying to the Lord Jesus, there should be no concerns about variety and change.

One church adds baptisms to the main Sunday morning worship service because they have found it has a huge impact on its evangelistic outreach. Baptismal candidates are encouraged to invite ten of their FRANS to their baptism. The church has had over fifty guests at times for these services because people want to see this significant event in the life of their FRANS spiritual journey.

Another church had a children's program with a strong drama and musical department, which put on a big musical once or twice a year. They had the children's department put on parts of their big upcoming play once a month, even in its developmental stages. This encouraged children, as well as parents, to invite their FRANS to see the children perform before the Lord. These always resulted in high attendance at the church services.

One small church found that baby dedications were wonderful times for people in the church to invite their FRANS. The church began spacing out baby dedications once a month and this provided a steady stream of new visitors that could be more easily assimilated than if all baby dedications were on the same day.

One church used special musical contacts to bring local, regional, and even national singers and groups into the church once a month to give a stirring solo or group performance. This proved extremely popular and allowed the parishioners to invite their FRANS on one of these Sundays.

One church found that recognition for local fire fighters, police, teachers, coaches, etc., was a huge way to allow their people to invite FRANS. The church would dedicate about ten minutes of the service to officially thank the particular group. They would be invited to stand or come on stage and/or be handed an award or T-shirt. They would be prayed over and thanked for their contribution to the community. This particular church added hundreds of people to their church through this once-a-month gratefulness approach.

One church used their pastor's vacations as an opportunity to invite experts in various fields to answer questions about Christianity and other hot topics. This proved so popular that the church regularly grew during the summer, and the pastor found a whole new group of fresh faces when he returned. Some churches have recognized that these special aspects of a worship service are the most effective when they are coupled with one of the five big days in church attendance — Easter Sunday, Christmas Eve, Mother's Day, local holiday services, and the fall service around the time change. Within the last few years, the Halloween-alternative candy night has become a bigger draw to the church than even Easter in some communities. These days can be planned and geared for even by a small church so that the people of the church will invite the highest number of their FRANS.

Whatever your church decides to do, consider what your congregation would like to see added to the worship service so they would feel compelled to invite others. How can the service be adjusted so that it is not just for people "in the know," but is also interesting and accessible to visitors and regular worshippers?

Non-Sunday Special Events

More and more people are not willing to make their first visit to a church be on Sunday morning. They have little or no idea what happens in a Christian worship service and have huge fears about cults and religious rituals. These potential visitors do not know what churches do and are not sure that churches can even be trusted. A growing number of churches are finding that it is very helpful to hold community events that allow people in the church to get a feel for the people and staff of the church. These community events can be of all different types and varieties, but they should be on the church's grounds and introduce people to the congregation and staff of the church, if possible.

Examples of these types of events are: Oktoberfest safe candy exchange for children around Halloween; hosting a carnival on church grounds; allowing the city orchestra to use the facility for a concert; setting up a booth at the local city or county fair; hosting an Easter egg hunt; fireworks on the Fourth of July; Compassion Fair for non-profit organizations in the region; craft fair; musical concerts; Easter or Christmas pageants.

One church's Christmas program was so popular that they performed multiple nights. Over nine thousand people were exposed to the ministry of the church through this special event.

One church used their Halloween Trunk or Treat candy exchange as a citywide event by holding it at the local speedway. They advertised it heavily and had games, prizes, bounce houses, and slides for the kids. This was so popular that everyone in the city knew of this church and looked forward to this event.

One church held an annual craft fair before Christmas where people in the community, who created various crafts, could display and sell them. This allowed hundreds of people who had never come to the church before get familiar with the location, ministries, and style of the church.

One church gave away food and clothing once a month to hundreds of people in the community. The church collected non-perishable foods all month to be given away on one Saturday a month. This proved so impacting that people throughout the region heard the good report about the church. Many people who were skeptical about "religion" in general were invited to participate in serving the poor on the same Saturday and got a whole new picture of the people and staff of the church.

One church held a potty-training seminar for young families. A Christian psychologist and the pastor taught segments of the class. Three hundred young parents showed up at the class. At the conclusion of the class, the pastor let the people know that he was a pastor and they were welcome to visit his church the next day. One hundred and fifty of the people in the class attended church the next day.

One church used a Valentine's Day Banquet to introduce dozens of couples to the ministry of the church. This proved so helpful to the evangelistic efforts of the church that it was a primary source of new people every year. Which Sunday morning worship elements can be added to your normal service to encourage people to invite their FRANS? Which special events or community outreach can your church sponsor that will allow people in the community to get to know the people and staff of your church?

3. Mass Media—Radio, Social Media, Television, Newspaper, Phone, Flyers, Direct Mail

Every church has to make a decision on the nature and level of their Community Awareness Strategy. Will you use mass media, and, if you do, to what extent will you dive into that type of Community Awareness? Some churches decide that this is a form of shouting it from the rooftops as Jesus commanded us. Other churches recognize word of mouth advertising as the only legitimate forms of publicity that is not tainted with deception and/or fear mongering.

If your church decides that any form of community awareness that does not come unsolicited from the mouth of satisfied Christians is inauthentic, then the next section should be skipped. If, however, your church is willing to see the mass media as a way of getting the word out about your ministry, then this next section might be of specific interest to you.

Radio

Radio ministries offer a wide variety of ways to get the word out about your church and its various ministries. Some churches use the free radio announcements that many, if not most, stations make available to non-profit organizations that are having an open-to-the-public event. Some churches move to the next level in radio ads and pay for a station to repeatedly air information about particular services, groups, or ministries that the church offers. Some churches will put these ads on Christian and non-Christian radio stations, depending upon their level of comfort with these various radio formats. If the event is highly evangelistic, it makes sense to try and get it to a non-Christian audience, who would be the most receptive. Some churches have sponsored high-profile Christian ministries as a way of connecting to an excellent ministry and riding the interest in that ministry.

One church spent all their community awareness monies to sponsor a national and international Christian program. They received more people visiting the church than they could adequately follow-up on, so they did not do any other community awareness. Some churches put their own pastor's sermons on the radio daily or weekly and saw a large number of visitors as a result. If a church is going to put their pastor on the radio, then it is important to put him in the best possible venue for his talents. That might be a call-in show; it might be a recorded panel discussion; it might be a back-and-forth show with a sidekick; it might be putting his sermons on the radio.

Social Media

More and more people are dependent upon social media to keep them informed and to let them know what their friends and acquaintances are doing. This area of networking, advertising, and connecting is crucial for a church to leverage. Without a Social Media presence, certain age groups will not know you exist. Reach out to various people in the church or in the community who know how to set up various social media accounts and how to advertise using this medium.

Television

Television ministries are being used more and more by churches to let the people in the community know of the churches' ministries. The same type of variety than can be used on the radio is also available in television. Some churches use stations' free ad space to let people know about their various open-to-the-public services and meetings. Some churches produce ads to be aired on local programming stations. It is possible now to purchase great looking ads from various Christian marketing companies.

These ads are well done, low cost, and effective. One needs to be the only one using the ad in your area. Some churches film their service and air it on a local access channel. Some churches film sermons and classes for replay on local television. Some churches create a talk show format or panel discussion or teaching venue for their pastor to let people know about the church and its ministries. Television is often much more expensive than radio and so clarity about what is trying to be accomplished is needed.

Newspaper

Newspapers have been effective for decades in letting people know about the services and ministries of the church. This community awareness medium is becoming less effective for reaching younger people, as they are less likely to look at a newspaper. They are used to getting all their information on the web or through radio or television. If a church uses the newspaper to increase community awareness, it is most effective if the ads are taken out for sections of the newspaper other than the religious section. If a church's ad appears with hundreds of others in the religious section, a person has to be looking for your particular kind of church to notice your ad. This kind of specific denominational affiliation is not happening much anymore. Many churches have found it more effective to pay a little more to have a clever ad in the lifestyle section of the paper or the sports section of the paper. Some churches have found that if their pastors will write opinion articles that are published in the paper about a variety of items, this results in far more people getting an idea about the church. These opinion articles may be letters to the editor, or actually published, more formal discussions.

Phone Solicitation

A number of churches have used phone solicitation as a way to get the community to become aware of the church. In some areas this has been a wonderful way to increase the community awareness of the church. In other areas, this has not worked well and has marked the church as a pushing place where "Pastor Mark" preaches—the one who calls and bugs us. Some churches have used parishioners to call all the numbers in a local area. Some churches have hired banks of people to get the message about the church out. Some churches use a recorded message from the pastor to let everyone in a region hear the same message. Some churches have conducted a survey on various topics to gauge interest and to show interest in community attitudes.

Flyers and Posters
A number of churches have used flyers and/or posters to promote church events. These flyers are often placed at local retailers and service organizations so that people can take a flyer to be aware of a specific event at the church. This form of community awareness works in certain communities but is often overloaded to the point where there are so many different flyers for civic organizations, churches, and clubs that they no longer draw attention.

Along with flyers, posters are a time-tested way of advertising about your church or a specific event. Posters need to be well done and must be eye-catching. They need to be changed regularly as any poster will stop being noticed after a few weeks. A poster must give clear directions to the event with accurate times. A poster needs to make the community aware of something that they would be interested in. Too often a church wants to make the community aware of events and ministries that only those inside the church are interested in.

Direct Mail
One of the most effective methods for making the community aware of a church and its ministries is direct mail. I have long

been an advocate of direct mail, as it touches people that have no natural connection to your church. At present, most churches suggest that direct mail with a tie to a website is the biggest draw of people other than FRANS. There are more and more companies that will help a church design and implement a whole strategy in regards to direct mail.

Most people responding to surveys like getting mail, even if it is junk mail. Direct mail has a positive impact, because it can be reviewed at the person's leisure and discarded or accepted without any uncomfortable interaction. Some churches send out direct mailers once every month just to let the community know what the church is doing. Some churches send out flyers in advance of big services with special guests or special elements to the service. Some churches use blanket direct mail, which reaches every home surrounding the church. Some churches target their direct mail pieces to certain zip codes or certain zones in a city. If direct mail is used, then an excellent mailer is needed. Clarity is a must and a real need or interest must be touched upon through the advertising piece. At least three pieces of direct mail needs to reach its target over a period of time before they begin to remember the church and its ministries. Do not expect that sending one direct mail piece one time will cause the church to be swamped with people who need to be assimilated.

New levels of effectiveness are being obtained with direct mail by insisting that pictures of actual people in the church are featured on the direct mail piece. The senior pastor's picture and his family are also important so that people have a sense of connection with the pastor before they get to the church. Many direct mail firms are now saying that for any direct mail flyer to be effective, there has to be a great looking website behind the church. If the website is not up to date with a pleasing look and feel, then there is no point in doing the direct mail flyer. Most people now will go on the web to find out more information about the church if they are intrigued by the flyer and before they visit the church. The flyer just gets them to visit the website.

Door-to-Door
Down through the centuries, door-to-door canvassing of an area has been the most utilized method for inviting people to the church and letting people in a community know about a church. This method can still be effective. Some churches use door-to-door canvassing to pray for every house in a region once a year, while hanging a door hanger on the door of the home. Some churches train up teams of people to evangelize people through constant door-to-door witnessing projects. Some churches train people to go door-to-door to let people know about various ministries that church offers and to answer questions about the church, but not to evangelize. If a church is going to use door-to-door canvassing of neighborhoods, this needs to fit with their style, and it needs to be a long-term strategy. A one shot door-to-door strategy does not create a lot of people visiting the church. It works over time as people realize that these people will be back to tell us about what they can do for us.

Event Promotion
If you are going to use the media to promote the services and ministries of the church, it is important that you highlight the ministries that meet an obvious felt need of the community. These would include marriage, parenting, child-care services, gratitude to civic servants, understanding the supernatural, etc. If the community is going to come to the event, then it must make sense to them, and it must be about a topic, ministry, or service they would be interested in. When you host an event like this, congregants need to be very aware of new visitors and be careful to not talk about things that only interest church people.

4. Website — Current, Relevant, Picture / Video Rich, Informative
To be taken seriously a website is a must. Most people, if they want to really check out a store or organization, expect that there will be a website to get all of the details that one used to have to go to the actual location to receive. People expect to have all their questions answered in an engaging way on the website, and they can get a sense from the website whether it is their kind of church. They get this through the pictures posted on your site, the humor you use, the activities you choose to announce, the colors, speed, and types of articles on your site.

A website is a must these days to reach out into the community. Realize that in the past, if people received a flyer or an invitation to a church, they might take that invitation to the church with them. Now they take any invitation and/or interest in the church to the website to check out the church before they would ever go to the actual church. Therefore, if the website is not helpful, inviting, and easy to navigate, they will never make it to the church. This is where the newsletters are now being posted and where information is sought about your church and/or ministry. Many youth groups should be given a separate website that is not connected except by a link to the main church's website if non-Christians are trying to be targeted by the church. The teens of today do not want to be a part of a pull-down menu of an organization that they don't know about and probably don't trust. They want to go straight to a stand-alone website with cool images and cool music.

If a website is being used properly, it is changing every week so that people can repeatedly visit the front page of the site to get new information. The more youth-oriented the site is, the faster the site has to change, daily or hourly in some cases. Answers to prayer, prayer requests, articles, pictures, blogs, reactions to editorials, sermon notes and sermons, small group outlines, etc. can all be posted to make sure that the site is constantly changing. In many churches, they are asking a person at every event or activity of the church to be a digital photographer and post those pictures so that people will visit the site and get the other news, also. The website is a great way to let people know about your church, as long as your site is interesting.

5. Signs — Excellent, Noticed, One Half-Step-Up in Class

Most churches do not consider what their signs tell the community about their church. But their sign says all kinds of messages to those who might visit. It can say whether this is a group who values excellence. It can say whether the church is modern or traditional. It can say whether the church is negative or positive. It can say whether the church is stuffy or friendly. It can say whether the church is open to non-believers and seekers or is only for Christians. It can say whether you already have to understand the particular lingo and beliefs of this group, or whether newcomers with no background in this type of church can come.

Signs say all of this by how they are constructed, what type of materials are used in the sign, the size and style of the letters, the messages on the sign, the tone of the messages on the sign, how prominent the denominational tag is on the sign, etc.

Be careful not to have a sign that says things you are not trying to communicate. I remember one church building, which you could not see from the road, had a terrible sign. The sign was a 4 X 8 sheet of plywood, which was weathered and bending out on the upper left-hand corner of the plywood. It had a fading picture of Jesus from the 1970's, who was smiling and saying that the church was just up the hill around the corner. I remember having an image of this old, dilapidated church building that looked as bad as the sign. But to my surprise, I was shocked that this modern, well-maintained, large church structure was there instead. The sign sent all the wrong messages.

Once a sign is erected, many people forget about it; but often the sign is the main way that people hear about the church and initially make their decision whether they are going to visit that church. I remember one church had a sign on a main road where thousands of cars passed every day. The pastor had the youth pastor take care of the sign and he put clever little sayings up every few days. People would always laugh at the little sayings that were up on the sign. The church had a steady stream of people visiting the church because of the sign, but no one stayed, because while the sign and the youth pastor were endlessly humorous, the senior pastor had no sense of humor at all and always preached hell-fire sermons.

6. Newsletters — Email, Snail Mail, Positive, Interesting
The church newsletter is still effective in certain settings, although much of it is now handled by email or electronically. Every cost effective way that the church can get its message and presence into the community should be explored. Most people today have an email account and so the church should have a weekly bulletin or information that goes out on the blanket email so that everybody gets all the news. A mailed newsletter can still be very effective if it is filled with interesting things to read.

The key to any newsletter is that there needs to be at least one thing in the newsletter that people will want to forward on to others—an interesting fact, a tear-jerking story, a different take on the news, news that no one else has, etc. If there is nothing in the newsletter or email that is worth saving and passing on to others, people will quickly stop reading it or handing it to others. The email is a way for many pastors to send something to their parishioners every day that will make a difference in their lives. It is making the possibility of shepherding the whole congregation easier.

7. Buildings, Grounds, and Parking — Guest-minded, Accessible, Clean, Color schemes, Flow

In many cases, your physical location and appearance of your buildings is the loudest megaphone into the community about the style, nature, and openness of your church. The building itself will be seen and noticed by everyone. Therefore, it is sending a message. I remember one church where the parking lot was allowed to grow weeds at least a foot high.

The pastor did not think it was his job to do it, so he did not even concern himself that it was not being done. I remember when he wondered why no one ever visited the church. If your church looks like a funeral home (many older churches have that look), then people will not be going there unless they have to. You need to consider things from a visitor's point of view. Is it obvious how to park and get into the service?

In many churches, it is not and people feel embarrassed to ask where the main auditorium is located. Is it obvious from the parking lot where the children's and teen activities are located? I know of a few churches that have spent money to renovate the front of the church and have seen a significant increase in the amount of visitors who are drawn to the updated look of the church. This is the big take-away from this section. Your building is a huge billboard shouting to the community what your church is like. Make sure that the building is saying what your church is really like and that you want people to come and visit.

It would be very helpful for many pastors and church leaders to have different unbiased people drive by your church and tell you what they thought the church was like just from the building, grounds, and parking lots. Often a church can significantly increase their attendance if they just clear away the shrubbery and paint the church a brighter, more modern color. Some churches that have moved to a more visible location have grown significantly, because more people see the building than before.

If your church facilities are hidden, then your church facilities are hindering people from knowing that you are open for business. If you are in a school or warehouse or theater, then you must rely on signs and other means of letting the community know that you exist.

The parking lot is another issue in many churches these days. People want to have easy access and egress from the church. If it looks like they might get trapped in the parking lot, new visitors might not want to come. Is there a clearly marked visitor parking area that is in a prime location? This will send the message that the visitor was expected and is given preferential treatment. If the parking lot is over 80% full on peak times of church facilities use, then it is time to do something about the parking problem. Even if the church building is not full, but if the parking lot is

80% full, then you will begin choking off growth. I remember one family drove into our parking lot for one of our services and could not find a spot in our parking lot. They drove out never to return. I was heartbroken over the fact that we were not able to minister the gospel to them because we had too few parking spots. After that, I required all the people who could to park on the dirt lot next to the church so that there would be room for everyone who wanted to come to the service.

Which of the preceding **Community Awareness Strategies** are you already employing? Which ones are you going to add to your church this next year?

What will your church do to attract people to come?

	Needed	Cost	Time	Approval	Person
Word of Mouth					
Personal Invitation					
Direct Mail					
Social Media					

COMMUNITY AWARENESS STRATEGY

	Needed	Cost	Time	Approval	Person
Phone					
T.V.					
Radio					
Billboards					
Signs					
Flyers					
Door to Door					
First Impression Piece					
Website					
Building/Grounds					
Other					

Chapter 2

First Visit Strategy

A new family decides to visit your church this Sunday. What will happen? Ideally, as they walk toward your auditorium, another friendly couple will say hello to them and maybe shake their hand. As they approach the main entrance, they will see an information booth with smiling people ready to assist them if they want specific information. Just before they go into the auditorium, someone reaches out to shake their hand, smiles at them, and welcomes them to the church. As they enter the foyer of the church, a warm and smiling usher will reach out to shake their hand and hand them a bulletin and offer to escort them to their seat or to the children's ministry area if they have children. While they are walking back to the children's area with the usher, they will engage in pleasant conversation about their family, religious background, and/or residency in the area.

The usher introduces them to the appropriate children's worker, who welcomes them to the class and offers to show their child around the room, giving an overview of what will be covered in the class that morning. The children's worker leads them to the place where they can fill out the appropriate registration materials for leaving their child in the class. The children's worker thanks the couple for coming and letting the church minister to their child. Then the usher shows the couple how to return to the main auditorium and to an appropriate seat for them.

At this point, if the service has not already started, a host family for that section of the auditorium comes over to introduce themselves and welcome them to the church. The host couple makes sure that the couple has a bulletin and goes over what will happen that morning in the service. The host couple lets the new couple know that the church has a gift for them as a way of saying "thank you for visiting our church." The host couple gets the gift and presents it before the service. The service starts and the music and message are wonderful. During the announcements, a warm, funny, and engaging person leads the congregation through the new information that everyone needs to know. They also let the visitors know that the church has a gift for them. At this point, the visitors are encouraged to fill out the visitor registration card and the ushers hand them the gift and more information about the church.

After the service, the couple goes to pick up their children and they are warmly greeted as they work their way through the security and are handed information about children's ministry or a family devotional to do at home. As the couple head back out towards their car, they are greeted and thanked for coming by a warm and friendly individual near the parking lot.

How close does this compare to what your church does for visitors?

An effective assimilation strategy hinges on the experience that the guest has on their first visit. If they were welcomed and felt the love of the church and the Lord Jesus Christ, then they have a much higher likelihood that they will be back the next week. Many churches just count on the friendliness of their people to let the new people know how loving and compassionate the church is. It is far better to plan on how the people of the church will demonstrate the love of God to the guests.

Too often, when a good first visit is left to chance, it is left to the pastor personally or to chance. When a church is small, it is appropriate that the pastor or one key lay couple do most of the welcoming of visitors. But as a church grows, it is crucial that there be adequate planning and a team.

It has become common knowledge in healthy church circles that only 16% of the visitors who come once to your church will eventually become a member of the church. But if a visitor comes two weeks in a row, then the likelihood that the person will become a member of the church grows to 85%. Therefore, it is crucial that the church do a quality job of encouraging the visitor to come back the next week.

Three First Visit Strategies

Three things must take place to give the best chance of having a great first visit. **First**, they must be loved in six crucial zones of warmth. **Second**, they must be given all the information that they need to understand the ministries, mission, and manner of the church. **Third**, they need to be given the level of personal sovereignty that they need.

1. Six Zones of Warmth — Embrace Them Six Times with Christ's Love

As the story at the beginning of this chapter illustrates, there are six zones of critical warmth in a person's first visit to the church. If the visitor senses that they are greeted warmly and accepted in these six zones, they will most likely make a decision to come back the second week. In each zone—whether we want to admit it or not—people are deciding whether they will stay and whether they will come back. It is often the woman in a family who makes that decision, but decisions are made based upon the information received in those six zones. What are these six zones of warmth? They are:

1. The parking lot
2. The front door
3. The lobby, foyer, bathrooms, courtyard
4. Children's classrooms
5. Main auditorium
6. Exiting the campus

Churches need to evaluate whether they have a plan to be loving, friendly, and encouraging in each zone. People largely have a sense of how welcoming, friendly, and loving a church is by how they are treated and/or anticipated in these six zones on the church campus. Do not leave to chance or rely on hoped-for-friendliness when with a few thoughtful actions the church can be perceived as clearly warm, friendly, and loving.

ZONE #1: Parking Lot — Parking lot attendants, assistance, signs, and buildings

How do you create warmth and acceptance in the parking lot for people who are visiting? One of the first ways to create warmth and friendliness is to station people in the parking lot to shake people's hands as they are headed to the church facilities. I used to ask people to go back out to their cars a few times before the service started and greet people as they walk back in each time. Having a special section of the parking lot cordoned off for visitors in the prime places to park makes visitors feel privileged and it helps identify who the visitors are.

If the church is large with lots of cars coming in and out, then parking lot attendants directing traffic are important to have in place to improve the organization and experience of the people as they are coming to and leaving the church. Assistance for the elderly or disabled is also good to have. Having signs on the buildings that clearly indicate what that building is used for and where the main entrance is can relieve anxiety. Many people are very anxious as they get out of their cars to head to a new church—both Christians and especially non-Christians.

Having all of the above ways of being friendly, warm, and accepting says to the visitor that they were expected and welcome. The goal is to take away anything that could embarrass them.

ZONE #2: Front Door — Greeters, friendliness, cleanliness

How do you create warmth before a person goes into the building? Warmth, friendliness, and acceptance are most often created before a person goes into the building by using greeters outside the building. These people need to be friendly, helpful, and genuinely care for the people who will be attending the church. They need to greet everyone who comes into the building, not just the new people. They need to help people find their way to the various sub-ministries if there are questions. They may need to help people keep out of the rain, snow, or wind in certain parts of the country.

If it is appropriate to be outside because of weather conditions, then an information booth that is plainly visible from the parking lot placed near the front door is helpful. The information booth can have coffee and donuts to encourage people to stop by. It needs to have knowledgeable and friendly people manning the booth, whose focus is attending to the needs of the visitor, not their friends at the church. Cleanliness of the area is also important. Trash and clutter are distracting and give the sense of disorder and a non-caring attitude. The goal is to make them feel like they are visiting someone's home; that they are experiencing the hospitality of someone who cares about them and is prepared for their visit.

ZONE #3: Lobby, Foyer, Bathrooms, Courtyard, Sitting Areas — Ushers, information booth, runners, cleanliness, pictures, food and beverages

Another zone of warmth is inside the lobby/foyer, the bathrooms, and/or any courtyards or sitting areas. The new guest is finally inside the church building and they need to sense that this is a warm, accepting, and welcoming place. Remember that they are making judgments all the time about whether they fit in this church. It is important to match the appropriate cultural ways of being friendly and warm. For some communities it is hugging and for others it is a handshake. For some communities there are cleanliness standards that are well above the average cleanliness of large assembly situations. Visitors are making decisions based upon sights, sounds, smells, and feel of the lobby. If the lobby doesn't have a welcoming feel, then they are less inclined to come back. It used to be that the styles and colors in a building changed every twenty years or so, and then it was every ten years, and now it is closer to every five years. Inside the lobby/foyer, the usher is waiting to be a pre-evangelist and ambassador of the love of Christ in how they greet and hand the person a bulletin. They must greet the person with warmth and focus. Too often, ushering is seen as an unimportant job, but in many churches, the usher is the make-or-break person for visitors. The usher is a pre-evangelist praying for each person as they hand a bulletin, expressing the love of Christ through their eyes and words and handshake.

The lobby/foyer should have lots of pictures and invitations to participate in various ministries. The younger the person, the more video- and picture-rich the environment needs to be. It should be a place of beauty and life. While it needs to be a place for some churches to keep winter coats and boots, it should not smell or be disorganized. Some churches have found that having coffee served in the lobby and small round tables at which to stand or sit is a very attractive and warming element of the normal lobby/foyer. In fact, many churches have significantly warmed up their lobby by making it have the look and feel of the local Starbucks coffee house.

If the climate of the church outside does not allow the information booth to be outside, then some form of information booth or table in the lobby/foyer is needed. There needs to be a place where people can go and ask questions and receive accurate answers. If you don't provide this service, then some people will feel as though you did not anticipate their visit or they will get the wrong answer from someone they ask.

In some churches, there are runners who the usher can assign to take the new person to where the children's classes are located. In some churches, it is easier to have the usher take the person and have another usher step in and start handing out bulletins and greeting new visitors.

The bathrooms, especially the ladies bathroom, are far more important than many think. A number of years ago I was giving a seminar in a southern city and a senior pastor said that he served a church that was over one hundred years old. It looked like it, too. A lot of what I suggested in this book, he said, would never be allowed. He didn't have much help and much budget. I encouraged him to work on the ladies bathroom, as this makes a huge impression when a visitor comes. The senior pastor and the associate pastor completely remodeled the main women's restroom. They put in new mirrors, new lights, new furniture, new paint, and the like. It was a real showplace and extremely welcoming for the ladies. They did not tell anyone at the church that they were doing this makeover.

On the first Sunday after they did this, the adult Sunday School class that met next to the ladies restroom had the most unusual thing take place. A couple of ladies went to the restroom before the class started and were stunned when they walked in. They got so excited that they ran back into the classroom and grabbed a couple other ladies to see this miracle that had taken place in the bathroom. Then more ladies were told, and soon the whole class full of women was in the restroom. Then the men wanted to know what was going on so after making sure it was safe to enter, they let the men tour this miracle of the bathroom. It created a huge stir in the church, so much so, that some ladies started to invite their friends to church to see the new bathroom at the church. They had never invited friends to hear the sermon, but they were willing to invite people to see the new restroom.

The leader of the Sunday morning class started to look at the shabby way that his classroom looked; and he, at his own expense, painted and fixed up his classroom. I understand that the whole church eventually was updated and remodeled to "match" the bathroom. Remodeling a bathroom actually led to a mini-revival of interest in the church, in evangelism, and in doing things with excellence for the Lord's work. Realize that people are getting clues all the time as to how valuable your faith in God really is in your life. If you are willing to put up with seedy, outdated, and even smelly surroundings where you practice your faith, then it is obvious that your faith is not that valuable to you. This is especially true if you would not put up with that in your own home.

The most crucial areas in determining the experience for people on their first visit are the lobby/foyer, the ladies restroom, and the nursery. The cleanliness, order, and nature of these areas speak volumes to the ladies making these kinds of decisions.

ZONE #4: Children's Classes — Pleasant teachers, organization, security, and cleanliness

In many households it does not matter whether the parents enjoyed the service; it matters whether their children want to come back and whether the children's department was a place of trust and warmth to them and their children. Churches often underestimate the power of the people running children's ministries. Their friendliness, organization, and unhurried nature send a huge message to the people who will be putting their children in that ministry. If the people are too brusque or too disorganized or too hurried to spend time being friendly and welcoming to new people, then the church will often lose this family.

Many churches would do well to have training classes on how to interact with children and their parents before and after class. These few minutes at the beginning and at the end of the class, with both the young people and the parents, are the most lasting impression of the church.

Have a bright, organized classroom that is at the right temperature for the area. Have a friendly face at the door of the classroom. Conduct tours of the class and the whole children's ministry department on Sunday morning so that visitors can get a feel for the whole ministry. Encourage teachers and assistants to greet children and parents warmly as their willingness to hear more of the gospel may be riding on it.

ZONE #5: Main Auditorium — Hosts and hostesses, ushers, invitation to participate, smiles, and directions

The main auditorium is crucial to the overall impression and greatly influences the decision of whether the person and their family are coming back to the church. Realize that people make this decision after they have made lots of other decisions to even get to the place where this decision will be made. A church can plan to give the visitors a warm and welcoming experience of the love of God during their first visit.

Before the visitor even gets settled in, a host and hostess of the section that they are sitting in can come over and greet them again and make sure that they are comfortable and have had their questions answered. The host and hostess can let them know about the gift that the church wants to give them. The host and hostess can give them a gift. The host and hostess can give them a brief overview of what the service will be like: "The band will come out and play a few songs and then someone will come out and officially open the service in prayer. Then, we will sing a few songs; feel free to stand or sit during this part. Then we will have Scripture reading. We then take an offering, but you don't need to worry about that; it is only for folks who regularly attend. Then comes the message from the Bible, which is always really good and practical. After the message we have a few announcements and the service is over." One church I know does this verbal run through in the service so that everyone is ready for worshipping the Lord, including the visitors.

The songs, the announcements, and even the message should say to the visitors that they are welcome and this is an accepting place for people at various stages of their spiritual journey. Some churches, without meaning to, tell the visitor that they are not used to visitors and gives the message that it is a condemning place. When a church uses big Christian words, refers to people to contact but does not point those people out, or condemns people openly, the church sends the message that it is only for long-term members and those "in the know."

Another often overlooked part of warmth and friendliness is having announcements and activities in the service that are clear invitations for the visitor to participate. There is nothing as intimidating as being in a new place and not knowing what to do or when to do it or how to do it or even if you are allowed to do it. The leaders of the church and those leading the various elements of the service can choose to acknowledge that "there might be visitors with us today and we want them to feel completely free to jump in and participate as we do this next section of the service." Also saying things like "this next section of the service is just for those who regularly attend here and is not meant for visitors, so relax and don't feel that you have to participate." This can happen right before offering and alleviates a lot of fear in people's minds.

ZONE #6: Exiting the Campus — Visitor's reception, staff on hand, "thank you," parking attendants, welcome gift, invites to lunch, invites to participate, smiles, food and beverages, invites to conversation, offer gentle help

When a person visits your house, you never just stay seated and tell them "bye." All of us have been trained that it is important to be loving as guests leave our home. We walk with them, thanking them for coming, making sure that they have all their belongings. In the same way, a church needs to make sure that visitors realize that we are very encouraged that they came, and they are welcome to come back. Just as there were greeters and parking lot attendants on the way in to the service, it is important to have these kinds of people being friendly and thanking people for visiting as they leave.

The larger the church, the more important it is to have highly organized parking lot attendants. They make a huge difference. These are the last people the visitor will experience before they leave the church. If they are smiling and friendly, it is a powerful witness to the welcoming nature of the church.

A church can also encourage the exit zone to be a place of warmth by having a guest or visitor reception area with food and drink for the guests. This provides a place for them to ask more questions. Many people are more willing to stay around if there is food provided. If the pastor will come to this area following the service, it heightens the interest of a visitor coming to this area. The visitor will get special one-on-one time with the pastor to ask questions and interact. A visitor reception area can have more brochures about the church with a knowledgeable person answering questions and talking about the history and mission of the church. Some churches have even found it helpful to have a well-done video about the church playing in the background that people can watch if they would like.

Some churches have made it a point to have someone in the church invite each visitor out to lunch after the service. In fact, at the church I served, we had a few couples on tap each Sunday, who were extremely gracious and hospitable and willing to take people out to lunch after the service. Even if the visitor declines the offer of lunch, they are encouraged that a couple from the church would invite them to lunch. Some churches assign people to new couples to call them and invite them back the next week and offer to sit with them in church the next week.

2. Information: Giving and Receiving

Giving to the Guest — bulletin, brochures, videos, audios, books, flyers, pamphlets, etc.
It is crucial for information to be exchanged on a person's first visit to the church. Those who come to the church need to receive all the information that they may need about the ministries, beliefs, activities, and causes of the church. This information forms

the basis of whether they will return to the church and how many points of contact they feel with the church.

The church should provide multiple different flyers, handouts, booklets, and bulletins for the visitor to leaf through. The church needs to be open about who it is and what it does so that people feel like they can get whatever information they are looking for easily. Some churches have racks of information on the various ministries in the church in the lobby where anyone can get the information. Most churches have the information in multiple locations so that those at the information booth, ushers, hosts, and hostess, etc., can hand information to the visitor.

The information should be as colorful, engaging, and interesting as possible. It should have pictures and borders, as well as tear-out sections to respond. Remember, your information is telling a lot about your church. If your information says boring, stale, wordy, and old school, then that will be how people will perceive you. It is better to hand a visitor a series of brochures than to give them a thin booklet or book with all the information in it.

Receiving from the Guest — Cards, sign-ins, parental permission, person-to-person, presentation
One of the crucial pieces of a good assimilation strategy is receiving information from the visitor. This needs to be done in as unobtrusive manner as possible. There should be multiple points where this information can be collected — at the information booth, by the usher who brings the gift for the

visitor and says, "Could you just fill this out so that we have a record of your visit?" or in the children's ministry area as a parent puts their children in the classroom area. The host and/or hostess can also collect this as they greet and get to know the folks and their interests. They might say, "Could you just fill this out so that we can connect you to the ministry I was just telling you about." Each of these contacts needs to be very low key and not pushy at all. If the person hesitates to give their information, that is fine; they may want to give it at another time. It is best to make collecting information a matter of routine and not a big deal. Some churches have everyone in the church fill out a card so that giving information does not seem different. Some churches pass a registration book down each row so that everyone fills it out each week.

3. Personal Sovereignty

A pleasant first visit to a church involves the church respecting the personal sovereignty of the visitor. I am asked all the time what to do with people who are clearly visitors but who will not give their information. I remind the pastor or lay leader who asks this question that all of us volunteer to visit a church, and we all come with a certain level of comfort surrounding our personal sovereignty. Since we have been in the church a long time, we know all about the church and trust it implicitly. We do not understand why an increasing number of people are not giving the church the information that we need to incorporate them into the church. Some who visit are willing to give all their information and intentions to the church immediately. Others are more skeptical and may not want the church to know anything about them until they have checked out the church first. The church must not be so insistent about directing and collecting information that it violates a person's sense of personal sovereignty. In fact, there is a growing distance between the average person in North America and church life. This distance causes more and more people to distrust the church. When they visit a church for the first time, it is an unknown process for them. A growing number of people who visit a church will not in any way declare that they are present or want to be contacted for three or more months. They just want to observe. They should be allowed to do this.

Most churches need to give ample opportunity for people to give them their personal information and to get involved; but if the person for whatever reason does not want to surrender that information or time, then it is okay. Even though personal information is vital to the incorporation of people into a church, the surrender of this information is the individual's prerogative. Let me give you a few examples of why people might not want to give their personal information.

I have known police officers and school superintendents and others, whose personal information was very delicate and could not just be given out. I have known people who have had churches or sales people hound them after they have filled out a card, so they are very suspect. I have had people who are being compelled by God to attend church, but they have all their lives been atheist or agnostic or hostile to church. I have had people visit the church with someone else's spouse (in the midst of an affair) and do not want people to know they are there. I have had people who are hiding from government, creditors, or others but who feel compelled to come to church and try and find God so they do not want to share their personal information. I have had women who are fleeing from their husbands who beat them and their first stop is church; but if they give their information and the church contacts their home, their husbands may be able to track them down.

All of this is to say that there are multiple reasons why a person might not give you their personal information. Allow a person to withhold their information for as long as they want. When they trust the leadership and the church, they may be able to give you the personal information that you need to connect them deeper into the life of the church.

If a church pleasantly offers to receive the visitor's personal information at multiple points, but is not pushy, this is usually received well. If the visitor does not want to give the information, then this is fine and not met with resistance. The church will have people who, for various reasons, will remain at some level of detached observation for long periods of time. Realize that there is a reason that is sometimes very complex. Allow people the ability to retain whatever level of personal sovereignty that they need to hear the life-giving message of the gospel.

What will your church do to insure a good 1st visit?

FIRST VISIT STRATEGY

	Needed	Cost	Time	Approval	Person
Traffic Control					
Parking Lot					
Buildings					
Signage					
Information Area					
Greeters					
Host and Hostess					
Ushers					
Runners					
Ministry People (friendly)					

FIRST VISIT STRATEGY

	Needed	**Cost**	**Time**	**Approval**	**Person**
Age Awareness – Children					
Youth					
Young Families					
Seniors					
Gifts					
Clear Instructions					
Ease of Connection					
Information					
Refreshments					
Exit Warmth					
Other					

Chapter 3

First Weeks Strategy

Bill and Suzie Saunders decided to visit your church for the first time this past Sunday. They enjoyed the service and their children liked the children's ministry. They had to really disrupt their normal Sunday morning routine to get themselves and the children to church. They are not sure the hassle was worth it. They also don't want to jump into the first church they visit. They have a few others they want to try out as well as yours. What does your church need to do during this crucial first week after their initial visit to compel them to come back this next Sunday? If you are like many churches, you will just hope and pray that they come back. And you might send them a letter thanking them for their visit. There is a whole lot more a church can do to encourage Bill and Suzie to come back this next week.

After a visitor comes to the church for the first time, the first week is the most crucial time within the first six months to receive interaction with the church. If the church handles the first week well, the church will increase from 16% of the visitors joining the church to 85% of people joining the church. The first 48 to 72 hours of that first week are the most crucial part of the first week. The actions that your church can take will pay rich dividends in people becoming a part of your church and God's forever family.

Week One Strategy

1. Gift in the Service
A part of your first week strategy is to let Bill and Suzie know that they are welcome to become a part of your church by the gift that you give them in the service. This gift should be valuable enough that they will recognize your respect for them. It is usually best to think in terms of spending between $5-$15, per family, on the gift. It is best if the gift stays in the home for a month before it is used up or discarded.

Let me hasten to add that the pastor's sermon CD is not a gift. I believe you should give them one, but do not consider that the gift. Some churches give a book. Some give a jar of jelly. Some give a gift basket full of various things. Some give the *Jesus* video or some other clearly Christian video. Some give homemade cookies or brownies. Some give a paperweight. Some give a book written by the pastor. These and hundreds of other ideas are possible. The gift just needs to communicate the right things to the visitor and be present in the home of the person for about a month.

If you give a prepackaged gift, there needs to be a sticker affixed to the gift that tells about the church. One church put a sticker on the back of a jelly jar: "A sweet reminder of your visit to First Baptist." Our church put a sticker on the back of the coffee table books that we gave out that included the phrase, "Come grow with us at Twin Lakes," along with our service times, phone number, and address. Some churches put a sticker or ribbon on the basket that the gift comes in because they know that the lady of the house will probably hang on to the basket.

For a while our church gave people some Danishes from the local bakery. We were a huge hit with the bakery and the families, but it was gone in less than thirty minutes and there was no reminder of their visit. Our church included with the gift a refrigerator magnet with our church logo and pertinent information. Most people hang their most important items on the refrigerator and the magnets are useful for this. If your church becomes a part of holding their important papers to the refrigerator, then you have a permanent place in their home.

2. Gift-Drop Team

After the service and before Tuesday evening, our church sent out a team of people to drop a second gift at the home of the visitors. The team was instructed not to go in but to just ring the doorbell and let them know they were from Twin Lakes and had a gift for the family. Then they were to hand the basket to whoever answered the door. This was not a long visit but was just to show appreciation for their visit to the church.

The response to this gift-drop team was phenomenal. People were generally shocked that we would get back to them so quickly after they had visited. The gift was appreciated, and the general attitude of thankfulness for their visit was a huge draw.

They probably went through great difficulty to get to church on Sunday. People feel special when you go out of your way to thank them for coming. Too many churches make people feel guilty for not having already come to church.

Again, it depends on what the church wants to give as a second gift. Our church gave a one-gallon tree because trees were very valuable in the desert. This is just a thank-you-for-coming gift; therefore, it may not have to be as expensive as the gift the church gave on the first day. Some churches give a plateful of freshly baked cookies. Again, there should be some way of noting that the church gave this gift. I just heard about a church that is giving out Starbucks cards worth $5 and/or I-tunes cards worth five songs. These are very clever ways of saying "thank you for coming." The sky is the limit.

These are the parameters for this gift-drop team: they are to be at a visitor's home no longer than five minutes; they are not to go inside nor witness to the people at the home about their need for Jesus; they are to leave the gift if no one is home; they are to include a little handwritten note in the gift to tell who and where the gift is from. This is a way of making it abundantly clear that you understand the sacrifices that these people made to visit your church and you are grateful.

Some churches have found that it is better to drop the gift off on Sunday afternoon when their visit to your church is still very fresh in their minds. Some have found that it is more helpful to drop it by on Monday or Tuesday evening. But there is almost universal agreement that it needs to be dropped off within 72 hours. If the gift is given after that time, it can feel like a sales call as the good feelings from their visit have faded.

3. Phone Call from Pastor or Volunteer

Our church found that a secret weapon in making the first week after a person's initial visit memorable was if the senior pastor placed a quick call to the people and thanked them for coming. Most assimilation handbooks will say that it is more impacting if a layperson in the church makes the phone call. However, I have done an unofficial survey to find out that in churches under a thousand people, it is far more impacting if the senior pastor of the church places those calls.

Many pastors do not like making these calls, so they seize on any reason to delegate the call to someone else. Some pastors do not like making the phone calls because they may receive all kinds of questions about the doctrine and or ministries of the church. These questions can be uncomfortable if the pastor feels that he must "sell" everyone on the church. When a person asks a question about the church, it is a great opportunity to tell people positively about the beliefs and ministries of the church.

If the visitors do not agree with the position of the church or were looking for something else from a church, this is a great time to get things out in the open. As long as there is not a condemning attitude toward what the visitor is asking about, this can be a great opportunity to explain the church's position and keep a person from joining a church where they do not really fit.

When I was a young pastor, I felt that I needed to convince everybody that they needed to come to our church or else I wasn't a good pastor. So I would be personally offended if they did not end up agreeing with me or attending our church. As I grew older, I began to see that there were wonderful people, who loved Jesus Christ, but did not like the style of church that I was building. It didn't make them bad people because they were not exactly like me. I learned that I could save the church a lot of headaches if I encouraged people to find a church that would minister to their needs in the style or theological context they wanted.

One of the most freeing sentences I learned to say to all visitors was, "We want to help you find where God wants you to be. If God wants you at our church, then so do we. If He wants you at another church, then we want you there, also." I found that so many people appreciated this "open" way of thinking about their church attendance that lots of people on the edges of enjoying our church's style and core beliefs stayed, because they felt the freedom to leave.

I would usually make these phone calls on Sunday afternoons or in the early evening. Each call would last between thirty seconds and ten minutes. I would have a stack of cards on my desk at the church, and I would begin to call the numbers.

It usually went something like this:

> "Hello, this is Pastor Gil from the Twin Lakes Community Church."
>
> *(wait for response)*
>
> "Is this Bill or Suzie?"
>
> *(wait for response)*
>
> "I just wanted to say thank you for visiting our church today."
>
> *(wait for response)*
>
> "I hope you enjoyed the service today."
>
> *(wait for response)*
>
> "Did you have any questions about the service or about our church that I might try to answer?"
>
> *(wait for response)*
>
> "Thank you again for visiting our church."
>
> *(wait for response)*
>
> "Good-bye and may God bless."

4. Pastor and/or Church Letter

A well-written church letter that stresses how the church is ready to assist the visitor with their issues, needs, and interests is also very helpful. Most churches send out a letter to visitors, which is good. Sometimes churches use the letter to brag about how wonderful they are instead of focusing on the visitor and what they might be looking for in the church. It is even worse if the letter thanking the visitor for visiting is a puff piece all about the wonders of the senior pastor.

Write a letter that is about the church's desire to help the person in their spiritual journey. It should speak to the interest of the visitor, such as youth groups for their teens, children's classes for their elementary kids, places for mom to connect to other ladies in the area, excellent nursery care, men's activities that might be of interest to men, etc. The letter should be positive rather than negative, and hopeful and encouraging, pointing to a brighter future with the church involved in their lives.

Write a letter that tells how people just like them have been helped and touched by the ministries of the church. Include testimonials about the church from real people in the church. Make it personal, using their name in the letter in a few places. Make sure the letter is on quality stationery and not copied off from a form letter.

The following is a sample letter that is an example of the principles we have been talking about:

> Dear Bill and Suzie,
>
> I wanted to thank you again, in writing, for visiting the Twin Lakes Community Church this past Sunday. I realize that getting everybody ready for church on Sunday morning is not always easy. We are honored that you came by and wanted to check out our church. We are here to help you and be an encouragement and support to you. I do hope that you enjoyed the service this past Sunday and that the message was practical, informative, and comforting to you personally.
>
> It encourages me to meet new people like you who visit our church. We at the Twin Lakes Community Church are a growing church helping people find God and friendship in the Rift Valley. Some people let us help them in their spiritual journey to a deeper connection with God. Some let us help them with programs for their teenagers or their elementary-age children. Others let us help them connect to ladies in the community that they may not have met yet. And some allow us to get the guys involved in softball or fishing or other active events. Whatever we can do to encourage you, I do hope that you will not hesitate to let us know. I have included a full calendar of the various programs and activities that our church directs so that you can get a clear picture of whether anything would be of interest to you.

We are a church full of hope and excitement! God has been working through the people in this church for years to help them with the pressures and strains of life. Just listen to Sam and Darlene: "Twin Lakes really has been a great church for us. Our marriage was in real trouble when we first came, but through the classes and prayer, we have made a complete turnaround."

Listen to Don and Beverly: "We were attracted to the church because of the children's program. Our daughters just loved coming and learning the Bible and playing the games. We have met so many other people just like us at Twin Lakes. It has brought our family closer to God."

Donna says, "I wanted to start coming to church because our babies needed God in their life. Little did I realize how much my husband, Jim, would enjoy all the men's activities. He has made so many friends and is doing so many fun things, I practically have to pull him away from church."

We are encouraged that you visited our church and we have had the opportunity to meet you. We do hope that you will come back. This church is full of folks just like you who are pursuing God together and encouraging one another along the way.

In His Service,
(Pastor Name)

You want this letter to arrive at their house on Tuesday, Wednesday, or Thursday. It is usually one of these days that they will make the preliminary decision whether they are coming back the next Sunday. This letter is one more way to touch people with love and seek to introduce them to the loving God.

5. Visit, Lunch, or Snack with the Pastor
Some churches have found that setting up special times for visitors to meet with the pastor at a Starbucks, a popular bookstore, or restaurant can significantly connect people to the church. One of the churches that I work with started offering lunches with the pastor for new visitors. This was such a hit that they saw their assimilation rate soar to 93% when the pastor agreed to two lunches per week with visitors.

I know of one mega-church pastor who still does this kind of meet-and-greet meeting at a local snack shop every week. He feels that it allows him to get to know the people in his church on a more personal basis. When he does this, the visitors are shocked that this mega-church pastor would spend thirty minutes with just them. He gets the chance to find out about them and for them to hear his vision straight from the horse's mouth. He says that he always schedules these meetings away from church at a Starbucks or snack place. This allows him to leave when the time is up and to get outside the church environment.

What will your church do in the first week after the first visit?

	Needed	**Cost**	**Time**	**Approval**	**Person**
Gift in Service					
Gift Drop					
Phone Call					
Letter					
Visit					

The following is a sample card, which was circulated through the various stations of the Assimilation Team. Each column needed to be checked so that we could see these visitors were loved on sufficiently.

Assimilation Team Progress Card:

	Gift in Service	Gift Drop By	Pastor Call	Church Letter	Visit
Name:					
Address:					
City:					
Phone:					
Staff Phone Call	Specific Ministry Brochure	CO Group	Invitation Newcomers Dessert	Newcomers Dessert	

Comments:

Week Two Strategy

For years we struggled with how to determine if someone had actually come a second or a third time. We tried all kinds of ways to track this. We asked people to indicate if this was their second time or third time or fourth time. But this system did not work. We asked people who knew everyone in the church to stand at the back and try and notice who was a visitor. This did not work either. We tried keeping track of visitors who self-identified as being visitors. That did not work. We were trying to determine when we should trigger actions that would help incorporate a person into the life of the church.

Finally, we just decided to assume that our first visit and first-week strategy had worked and that they came on the second Sunday. If they had not come the very next Sunday, then what we did would be considered as follow-up from their first visit. This worked so well I have been advocating it across the country for years.

1. Staff/Ministry Phone Call

In the following week after a person's first visit to the church, we would begin a second round of phone calls, letters, and brochures. On the second Sunday after a person's first visit, the visitor card on that individual would be put on the desk or in the box of the staff person or ministry coordinator, who might connect with their situation the most easily. If a family had teenagers, then the card would go to the youth pastor to do this second-week phone call. If the person had elementary children, then the children's director would make the phone call. If the person had expressed some interest in women's Bible studies, then the women's ministry coordinator would make the phone call.

The phone call from the staff or ministry person is just like the first phone call the week before that came from the pastor or volunteer. It is just more ministry specific.

> *"Hello, this is Misty Sparling, the women's ministry coordinator for Twin Lakes Community Church. Is this Suzie Saunders?"*

> (Pause for an answer)

> *"I just wanted to call and say thank you for visiting our church."*

> (Pause for an answer)

> *"I also wanted to answer any questions that you might have about the church in general or the women's ministry specifically. Do you have any questions?"*

> (Pause for an answer)

> *"Let me tell you about some of the exciting opportunities in women's ministry that we have coming up."* (Events, studies, get-togethers, etc.)

(Pause for an answer)

"Thank you again for visiting the Twin Lakes Community Church. We hope to see you again this week and at our upcoming women's event."

This phone call gives the visitor another encouraging connection with the church and a different perspective on the church's programs and ministry. This second phone call is often the most helpful and the most unexpected. After the hoopla of their visiting the church the first time has died down, this second phone call tells them that the church has not forgotten about them. It also connects them much more directly to a place of interest in the church. This second phone call "says" that this church really does care about the people who visit it. It "says" that this church is intentional about connecting and serving people. These messages do not go unnoticed.

One church grew from 400 to 2,000 with this kind of intentional, organized approach to loving people. Almost everyone who attended the church admitted that the preaching was not stellar, but they came because of the organization and the relationships that could be built through this church. This church was not built on great preaching but on loving people in an organized genuine way.

2. Ministry Specific Brochure

Since this is the second letter or mail piece that the church will be sending to the visitor, it needs to be much more targeted to what they would be interested in than the general letter of the last week. This means that the two phone calls that were made to the person should have picked up some of the specifics about what the person was interested in knowing about the church.

One of the questions that I am often asked is, "What if we don't have anything really happening other than Sunday morning?" This is time where the church exists on the dream of what the leadership has agreed upon to move the church toward. A children's brochure in these cases will major on what you would like the children's ministry to accomplish and be like in six months to a year. Be completely candid in the brochure about the fact that the youth group is small but emphasize the good points it does have and the plans that you all have for the youth group.

There should be brochures on the children's ministry, the youth ministry, the nursery ministry, the music ministry, and the adult ministry for every church with over forty people. As a pastor, sit down and pen these brochures for the people who visit. These brochures should give people a glimpse about the programs that the church is doing. They should be full of pictures so that people can get a feel for that particular ministry.

One church took this concept one step further. For every child that they have in their children's ministry, they have a barcode scanner number that is specifically assigned to that child. The parent must have that barcode to pick up their children after church service is over. This church went ahead and printed that barcode on a nice key-sized card that can be slipped on mom's key chain along with the supermarket super saver card. This barcode scanner number on the nice looking card with the church logo and name is sent to the family so that they are ready to check their child in and out whenever they come to church. This allows less hassle and it means that the parent has the church name on their key ring. This is a very clever way of saying, "Thanks for coming and we are expecting you to come back."

3. Invitation to Church Orientation Groups

New visitors need to feel as though the church is following their integration into the life of the church. This means invitations need to be sent once a month or once every two months to be a part of a church orientation group. This reassures the new attender that they are being thought about.

Near the end of the second week, a phone call, letter, email, or other contact can be made to let the person know when and where the church orientation class is being held. The invitation is itself an opportunity to love on the visitor. These opportunities are important. Some churches have a secretary in the office make these contacts. Other churches have a volunteer from the Assimilation Team make these phone calls or contacts. It does not matter as long as this represents a third and completely different person who has contacted the person in the first few weeks of their involvement in the church.

Our visitor card had this box to check so that we could see that the visitor actually was followed up in this way. This is a simple contact, but it is another opportunity to have people understand that they are one of you all. These people have been included and are being regularly informed.

Now some people will object that people do not want to be touched this much during the first few weeks. This is true for some people, and they will usually not fill out the contact information so that you cannot contact them anyway. The vast majority of the people want folks at the church to welcome them and show them how to get connected. This just seems like the way it should be done. The visitor can beg off acting on the information, but the contact has been made.

4. Church Orientation (CO) Groups
A further way of loving on people is having them attend a church orientation class. We will discuss this in much more detail in the next chapter, but suffice it to say, having a person learning in a friendly environment, with people who are also new to the church, and being given the chance to let people know them better really speaks volumes about how welcoming the church is.

Too many churches try and wait until there is a big class of new attenders so that the people will be impressed with how many people came. This is not what these classes are about. They are about connecting other people to the new attender. They are about getting their feet wet in small group life. Do not place the chairs in rows, but put the furniture into one big circle, so that everyone has the opportunity to talk.

I recommend that there be five classes that are each about one month long. This allows people to go without having to commit to going to Sunday School for the rest of their life. The CO groups should have a definite end date and time. At the conclusion of one of the classes, a week or two should be given as a break. If the church has the classes on a constantly repeating loop, then new people can jump in whenever they want since there will always be a class to attend.

5. Invitation to Brunch/Dessert Gathering
One of the final ways to let people know that you are thinking of them is to invite them to the newcomer's dessert at the pastor's home that will be taking place in a few weeks or so. Smaller churches may only need to do this gathering every quarter, but the date can still be pointed to and invitations made and/or sent. The invitation to this dessert gathering is in itself a way for the church to make contact with the new person and be helpful and loving. Send out the invitation or make a phone call within the first few weeks of a person being a visitor to the church. Do not bunch the invitations to the church orientation groups and the dessert gathering. Each of the contacts you pursue for something that will benefit them is a plus for the church.

6. Attendance at Brunch/Dessert Gathering

When the actual dessert gathering takes place, this is another way to encourage people. When the person attends this kind of gathering, keep it light but warm, letting people get to know the pastor and ask a few questions. Sometimes in our modern hurry-up society we don't realize that separate invitations and separate events can be lifelines of friendship and relationship to the person who is coming to church to find God and others who can walk with them through life.

I just recently talked with a pastor who does this newcomers gathering as a potluck so that people feel involved and so that they don't back out. He told me that having people more involved is crucial to having a successful group. After the meal, he will break out a simple board game (he likes OUTBURST™) that gets people talking and having fun. He then asks people to share how they heard about and came to the church. This further allows everyone to talk and share. Finally, he asks everyone to trade nametags with someone in the group that night to pray for that person. This church has nametags for all their functions. It really increases their friendliness level.

Newcomers Dessert
Informal Setting
Sharing why they started coming to (Church Name)
Hear from Staff
Philosophy of the Church: (Church Name) Strategy
Evangelism: We believe there are five important facts about Heaven.
Time to seek out staff of their area of interest
Food

What will your church do the second week?

	Needed	**Cost**	**Time**	**Approval**	**Person**
Phone Call					
Ministry Brochure/Info					
Gift					
Orientation					
Dessert/Brunch					
Other					

Chapter 4

First Year Strategy

"I know how churches operate," John sarcastically proclaimed. "You lavish attention on the first-time visitor and make them feel so special. Then when they come back expecting to receive continuing attention and focus, we are forgotten as there are always new people who are the first-time 'special' visitors.' Don't tell me that you are filled with Christ's love for the lost if it only lasts for a couple of weeks." John noticed that many churches' assimilation plans are inadequate because there is this belief that all we have to do is get people to visit the church once and then they will naturally want to come back again and again.

Sadly, John stopped attending church regularly because he found it more rewarding to visit lots of churches for the first time. Why do an increasing amount of people hop from church to church? Because they see greater value in being thinly connected to lots of churches rather than deeply plugged into one church.

It is true that some churches are only set up to track and love on first-time visitors. These churches' assimilation plan only extends to the first visit. As you have seen, and it will be demonstrated further in this chapter, there is so much more that can be added to the church's strategic plan for visitors. In fact, if the church does not have a specific action plan for working with those who are between the second week and the twelve-month point, your church will lose many great people who could have been a part of your church.

It takes most people about a full year to be fully assimilated into a church. The church must plan how they are going to ensure that a person who wants to be incorporated into the life of the church is actually plugged into the life of Christ and the life of the church. The average person in a church will take a considerable amount of time and energy to actually get plugged into the church. This means that the person has moved past just attending on Sunday morning. It means that they go to a Sunday School class and/or small group.

It means that they participate in special events that the church puts on. It means that they understand what the church believes and have embraced those same beliefs. It means that they understand how to have a real relationship with God and they have begun that relationship with God through Jesus Christ. It means that they have started to serve in the church because it is now a family they are a part of. It means that they are committed to learning more about this all-encompassing thing called the Christian life. It means that they have significant friends and relationships in the church that add joy and value and meaning to their lives.

This chapter will tell you how to aim at those biblical outcomes and begin accomplishing the much deeper assimilation that is needed to transform a life. It is important that we understand that what is done in this important layer of incorporation is not the whole of the Christian life, but it is crucial to a lifelong embrace of the full Christian life.

There are four things that are crucial to the assimilation or incorporation of new people into the church. First, new people must be *oriented* to the church culture, information, systems, and structure. Second, they must begin to participate in the *small group life* of the church. Third, they must begin to build *friendships* with the people of the church. Fourth, they must be allowed to *serve* and find their niche in the Lord's service.

In *The Purpose Driven Church* by Rick Warren, he uses a baseball diagram to illustrate Saddleback Church's discipleship approach. Christianity 101, 201, 301, and 401 are classes that provide steps forward in the Christian life. What many people do not really understand is that this is really an assimilation plan for new people during the first year of their involvement in the church. It's a strategic plan for connecting people to a specific church. These classes are not meant to be the whole of Christian discipleship; instead, they are introductions to the basics of Christian living.[1]

---

[1] Rick Warren, Purpose Driven Church, (Grand Rapids: Zondervan, 1995)

My church used the following assembly line illustration to diagram a clear first-year assimilation strategy. A person started on one end of the assembly line and moved to the other end of the assembly line. This concept helped people see that they had moved from Visitor to Attender to Member to Maturing to Servant to Ambassador. This is what we wanted each visitor to do. We were able to clearly show what was expected of folks who connected with our church. We were able to remind people of the expected movement every seven weeks because of new small groups starting every seven weeks.

A significant amount of the assimilation process of a person or family into a church takes place after the first two weeks of intense interaction and before a year has passed. The person or family will either be assimilated in this time or they will drop out of your church and move to another church or into spiritual inactivity. What does a church do to ensure that it assimilates its visitors during that first year?

There are four sets of strategies for a church to focus on: Church Orientation Groups; Learning and Fellowship Groups; Friendship Strategies; Service Strategies. Each of these combines to form the First Year Strategy. I will briefly explain each of these below, but then delve into each one in the subsequent chapters.

1. Church Orientation Groups:

These are certain types of groups that should explain the beliefs and procedures of the church. It is not just that the person needs to be educated about certain content that they did not

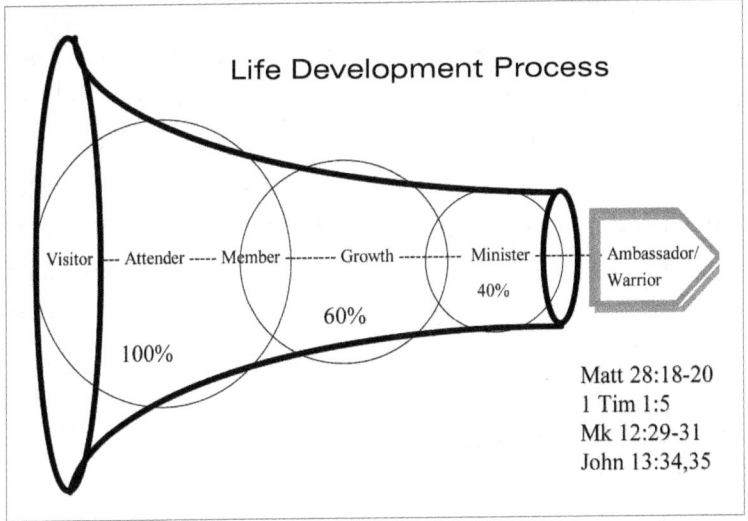

know before; they need to experience other teachers and people of the church, other than the Senior pastor. They need to share and listen and pray with other people in the church. They need to interact over their new growing knowledge of spiritual information.

2. Learning and Fellowship Groups:

A church that expects to assimilate new people must have new classes and new groups starting all the time. In this way they open the door for new people to be in on the start of something rather than joining as the Johnny-Come-Lately. Some people will want to be in a group where there is more focus on them talking about their thoughts, ideas, feelings, etc., while others will be more comfortable with content and lecture.

3. Friendship Strategies:

A church needs to provide a way for people to meet other people that they might become friends with. This friendship creation is one of the main reasons why people come to a church in the first place. There needs to be men's groups, women's groups, couples' groups, and family groups that aim at developing and deepening friendships. There needs to be events that allow a mixing of people so that new relationships might be formed. And there is a need for a wide variety of interest to be expressed so that people can find others with like-minded activities and thoughts.

4. Service System:

Having a short class in the first year that introduces the person to all the various parts of serving in a church is an excellent way to get people started with this crucial element in assimilating people into a church. There also needs to be service groups that they can join in order to do ministry together.

The church must have an intentional strategy to make these things happen during a person's first year of connection to the church. If these things don't happen in that first year, they will most likely not happen at all.

First Year Strategy Card:

Name:						
Address:						
City:						
Phone:						
	CO Groups	Foundations	Christian Maturity	Baptism	S.H.A.P.E.	Membership
	Content & Friendship Groups	CO Groups	University of LIfe	Sermon Based Groups	Women's or Men's Groups	Life Stage Interest Groups
	Friendship Strategies	Lunch	CO Groups	Service Groups	Friendships	Membership
	Service Strategies	First Serve Obsesrvations	Have to Service	Training		Want to Service

What will your church do during the first year to retain this visitor?

	Needed	Cost	Time	Approval	Person
Guest Area					
Food					
Staff Connection					
Job Opportunities					
Brunch/Dessert					
Beginners' Class					
Other					

FIRST YEAR STRATEGY

How will your church determine growing commitment?

	Needed	Cost	Time	Approval	Person
Church Directory					
Altar Call					
Baptism					
SS/BS Attendance					
Involvement					
Membership					
Other					

What will your church do to involve the attenders in the church's ministry?
1. Classes
2. Announcements
3. Recruiting
4. Ministry Fairs
5. Interviews
6. Yearly Commitments

How will your church cause people to sense the care, nurture, and love of your congregation?
1. Sunday School
2. Small Groups
3. Tele-Care
4. Visitation
5. Potlucks

Chapter 5

Church Orientation Strategy

"I really like this church," Jim declared, as he and his wife were leaving the church, "but I was raised Catholic and my wife was raised Pentecostal so we don't know how your church operates. My wife thinks this church is the perfect compromise between her upbringing and mine." They had been attending the church for a few weeks and were making all the noises that said they wanted to become a part of the church. I thanked Jim for his comment and realized that his question was exactly why we had five different classes that would orient him to our church. It would take that many different groups and classes to unpack their misconceptions about church in general and get him acquainted with the things our church did differently.

It is hard for many people in a particular church to recognize all the specialized things to know about the church they attend. It just seems that everyone knows these things. But it took them a while to know all the ins and outs of the church, and it will take a new person just as long, unless there is a foolproof education process that will bring people up to speed. A church orientation strategy is really a systematic way to bring people up to speed with what the church believes, how it operates, how to become a significant player, and why it operates that way.

A church orientation strategy must be a content transfer system so that anyone within one year of being at the church can play whatever role they are ready to play in the life of the church. Usually people will only give you six weeks to start on this process of orienting them to the church they are interested in. If you don't start something that will help them understand the way you all do church, usually they will leave. I have listened to dozens of pastors tell me that they have really sharp people or couples come to the church for a few weeks or a few months, but then they drop out just when we begin to notice them. This is tragic as a church has lost a potentially good member, and the person has lost a community of faith that they initially saw as so positive. This lag time between when a couple gives up on the church and when the church notices a couple is where the beginning of a good church orientation strategy should begin.

The church, the leadership, and the pastor must be ready to initiate the incorporation into the life of the church. It often doesn't happen because our churches have a mentality that is a holdover from the last few generations of church-going experiences. In the past when people went to church, we assumed that everybody was a Christian and that they knew all about how to be involved in church. We also assumed that when they wanted to get serious about becoming active in church, they would bring up becoming a member. All three of those assumptions are no longer true. Many people who visit a church are not Christian; they have little or no church experience, and they do not understand why they need to become members.

As I said before, Rick Warren has four classes: 101, which talks about the basics of membership; 201, which are the basics of a growing in Christ; 301, which are the basics of serving in that church; 401, which are the basics of serving Christ in the marketplace or the mission field.

Our church took a little different approach and held five different classes that visually moved people along an assembly line. We wanted to move them from visitor, to attender, to member, to mature Christian, to minister, and to ambassador/warrior. (See diagram for Life Development Plan in the Introduction.)

Our approach was to introduce five basic classes that lasted four to five weeks each throughout the year. Each one built upon the foundational blocks of the Christian life. They are: Christian Foundations Class, Christian Maturity Class, Baptism Class, S.H.A.P.E. Class, and Membership Class.

1. The Foundations Class is a class about the basic way to start the Christian life:

    Foundations Class
    Small group of people 8-20 max
    Sharing common info about each other
    New Life in Christ
    Understand the Bible
    Understanding God
    Understanding the Church
    Prayer Requests

2. Christian Maturity is a basic class about what becoming a deeper Christian entails:

   Christian Maturity Class
   Sharing common info about each other
   Evangelistic presentation
   Use fill-in-the-blank curriculum
   Orthodoxy: three-week brief overview of nine doctrines of faith
   Orthopraxy: three-week brief overview of ten relationships of life
   Take Prayer requests ... 1 per person
   Close in Prayer

3. Baptism Class is a basic class for understanding the meaning and significance of believer's baptism:

   Baptism Class
   Sharing common info about each other
   Evangelistic presentation
   Three New Testament pictures of Baptism
   Written declaration of Surrender to Jesus Christ
   Commitment of Baptism
   Baptism speech they will give (Personal Testimony)
   The operational procedures of Baptism

4. S.H.A.P.E. Class is a basic class for discovering your unique place in the church and mission in the world:

   S.H.A.P.E. Class
   Spiritual Gifts
   Heart / Passion
   Abilities
   Personalities
   Experiences

5. Membership Class teaches the remaining basics about the church's operation and key commitments that becoming a member entails:

   Membership Class
   Sharing common info about each other
   Evangelistic Presentation and Call
   Declaration of Surrender to Jesus and Church
   Philosophy of this Church
   Doctrine and Constitution of this Church
   Serving in this church ... Staff recruiters
   Giving to this Church

In the past, the membership class in many churches functioned as the church orientation strategy. It used to last thirteen weeks, or in some cases, six months. If you wanted to really connect with the church, then this was how you did it. What churches have found over the last twenty years is that very few people will sit through that many weeks of class just to be a member of a church. They don't spend that long learning about which insurance plan to become a member of, what gym to join, or what school to send their children to. The norm for information dissemination is one or maybe two meetings. What our church and many others have found is that if those classes are broken up into a number of shorter classes that constantly rotate, then people will attend them over the course of a year's time.

Rick Warren put together four classes that form the Church Orientation Strategy of his church in Southern California. He now does those classes on Saturdays. Each class takes four hours. During the class there are lectures, fill-in-the-blanks, discussions, homework, commitments, friendship development, etc. It usually takes people in his church about a year to go through all four classes. Technically they could do it in four months.

Whatever your church does, it needs to provide information and connections to people during the period between two weeks and one year so that a person is fully up to speed with how the church operates and what it believes. It is the most helpful if there are multiple teachers with different people attending each of the classes so that friendships can be built, care and compassion can be experienced, and questions can be asked and answered.

What will your church do to orient people to the church?

	Needed	Cost	Time	Approval	Person
101					
201					
301					
401					
Brunch/Dessert					
Foundations Class					
Christian Maturity Class					
Baptism Class					
Serving Class (S.H.A.P.E.)					
Membership Class					

Chapter 6

Small Group Life Strategy

The church must become one of the visitors' places of connection or they will never be assimilated into the life of the church. The church must be more than just a group of strangers sharing the same building and pastor. A church is a community of faith, and when done right, it results in the joy of sharing life together. A detailed discussion of how to connect people into small group life within a church is for another book, but the small groups of the church are a key element of the assimilation strategy of the church.

During the first year of a person's attendance in a church, they make the key decisions about how involved they will be in this church. If they make the decision to stay on the sidelines, then they may never b e truly assimilated even though they attend the church for years. To be truly assimilated, they have to do life with other people in the church. The church has to be one of the places that offer them support, encouragement, challenge, and comfort through the ups and downs of life. This does not happen on Sunday morning; it happens in small group life.

Successful growing churches constantly invite people into the small group life of the church. If these invitations constantly happen, at some point a person attending the church for the sermon and the worship crosses a line. That line is that these people, who were strangers before, are now friends — and even more — brothers and sisters in Christ.

Become strategic about getting people into small groups through invitations, monthly announcements, starting new groups constantly, providing sign-up sheets, introducing new, interesting groups, contact by leaders to people who show interest in their new study, setting end dates for small groups, and making the groups enjoyable and enriching.

Remember that the purpose of the church is to move people along the continuum of growth and development toward full maturity in Christ. Small Group Life is one of the most effective ways to do this process. People get a chance to care for one another; they get to share with one another; learn together; pray for one another; do compassion projects together, etc. It is essential that people be enfolded into small group life of some sort or they will not be truly assimilated. The problem is that you constantly must invite people to join new groups and new classes. People need to be pointed to growth and have easy points of entry into this growth process.

There are all kinds of different small groups that can be beneficial to the people of your church. These provide ways for people to connect with others, to be real, to grow significantly because of the accountability and care taking place in the small group. In the past, churches just had to provide classes on Sunday morning and this sufficed in providing the amount of small group life that people needed. Today, different kinds of groups are needed. The following chart will give an overview of eight different kinds of groups that churches today are using to minister effectively to people's needs. These different kinds of groups also form a significant part of the assimilation strategy of the church.

Eight Distinct Discipleship / Small Groups

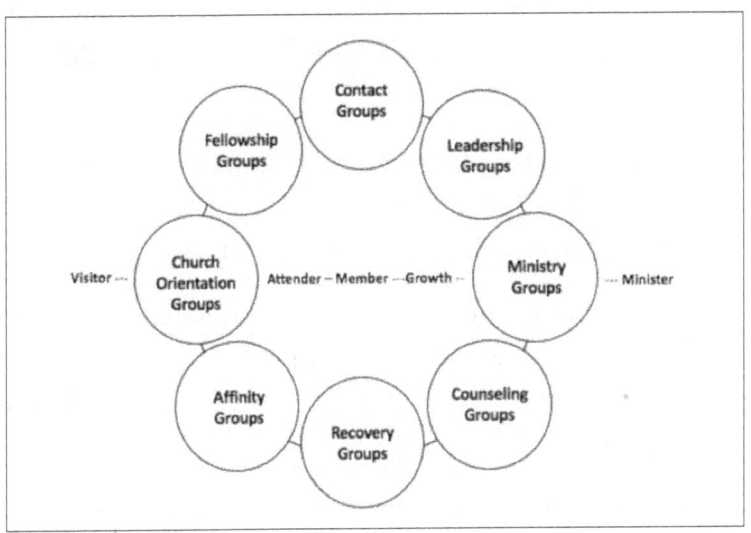

Usually one will form the core of the discipleship process in a church with the others orbiting around it.

Notice that these eight different kinds of groups allow people to move into deeper connection with the church along their own lines of interest and need. Let me give you an overview of these different groups:

1. *Church Orientation Groups* are made up of four to seven different classes that bring the person in a small group setting up to speed with the practices, beliefs, mission, programs, and core values of the church.

2. *Fellowship Groups* are often sermon-based gatherings for discussion, reflection, and application. Their key focus is 70% people and 30% content.

3. *Content Groups* focus on new biblical information and application. Their key focus is 80% content and 20% on people.

4. *Leadership Groups* are geared to potential leaders being trained to lead in a more Christ-honoring way. Their key focus is 80% people and 20% content.

5. *Ministry Groups* are for those individuals, who band together to accomplish a need in the church or in the community. Their key focus is 70% ministry and 30% people.

6. *Counseling Ministries* are for those people who need individual applications to solve their particular problems. Their key focus is 70% people and 30% content.

7. *Recovery Groups* are for those people who can be benefited by being placed in a group full of other people who are struggling with the same issues that

they are struggling. Their key focus is 70% people and 30% content.

8. *Affinity Groups* are for those groups of people who get together around a common interest or desire and spend some time exploring the Scriptures in addition to their interest. Their key focus is 50% affinity, 30% people, and 20% content.

Each of these different groups has a slightly different emphasis and orientation to small group life, but each difference is needed. The power of small group life should not be underestimated. Their purpose is to make people feel a part of a church. All of these different people will be coming to your church, and it will be important to allow the differences between people to be celebrated in these different kinds of small groups. You will notice that the focus of the different kinds of small group are different in the amount of time they give to letting people talk or having new biblical content shared and/or participating in ministry or a particular interest.

The point of small group life is to surround people with other people who will care for them, pray for them, support them, and encourage them. Most churches are finding that the real life of the church is in the small group and not in the large Sunday service. The large service is important, but the small group is so essential for the carrying out of a different level of worship, discipleship, evangelism, fellowship, and compassion.

In the church that I served, we used the content-oriented small group to teach the depth of the Christian life. We encouraged everyone to go through this three-to-five year curriculum that would give a robust understanding of how to be a full Christian. This provided content, friends, spirituality, and a common core Christian belief as they served in our church and lived their Christian life. People would go through this content in a small group over time, and they also had the other types of small groups available to them.

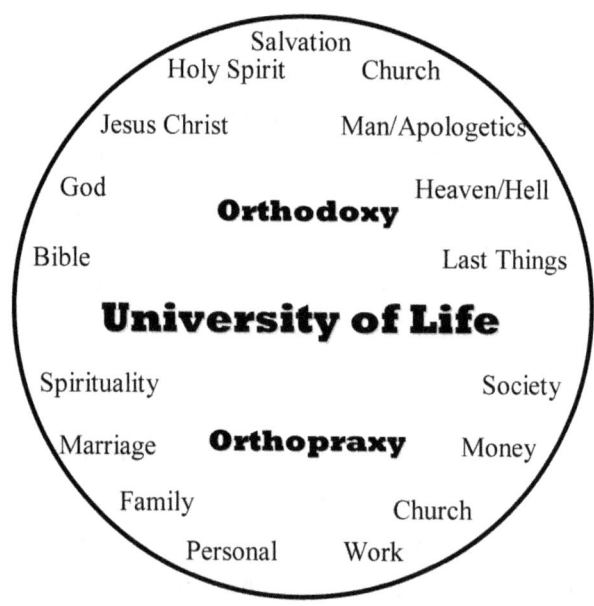

What will your church do to get people participating in small group life?

	Needed	Cost	Time	Approval	Person
Content SG					
Ministry SG					
Fellowship SG					
Recovery SG					
Leadership SG					
Affinity SG					
Counseling					
Church Orientations SG					
Serving Class					
Membership Class					

Chapter 7

Service Strategy

Pete and Samantha had only been in the church for three to four weeks when they approached me after the church service. Pete said, "We want to get involved; what can we do?" At that point in our church's history, we did not have a good plan in place to get people serving quickly, so I stumbled over my thoughts and words and said, "Let me get back with you." I was so used to having to beg people to get involved that I was taken aback by this amazing couple we knew nothing about, but who wanted to serve. At that time, we always needed people to teach children's Sunday School classes, but I didn't know if they were qualified or ready to do that job. I didn't know where they were in their spiritual journey, and I didn't know what their gifts, talents, and interests were. They eventually suggested that they could put in the tile work in the new building. This was a great blessing and got them involved right away. Most people are not as persistent or as discerning as Pete and Samantha. They knew that they needed to help out to really get to know people in the church. It is the church's job to help them get involved in the church for all the benefits that will come to them and all the benefits to the community and the church.

Realize that if you get people involved in serving the Lord, you benefit them far more than they benefit you. Most pastors have this "I don't want to bother people; they are already so busy" attitude. People are busy. Yes, it will involve major disruption to their lives if they begin to live a balanced Christian life, but it is a wonderful disruption. Serving the Lord pleases Christ; it connects people to each other; it allows you to hear more clearly from the Lord; it rebukes the selfishness and sin inside of you; it allows you to love your community; it allows you to use your gifts and talents directly for the Lord; it provides a deep satisfaction that few things can add to life. People need to be guided into service and shown how beneficial it is to their connection with God, to their friendships, to their self-esteem, to their balanced healthy life, to their community, etc.

People don't join churches to sit on the sidelines; they join churches to get involved. People who don't get involved are not really assimilated. Every church must invent a system to get people involved in a significant way within one year, or the person who arrived just a short while ago will quickly leave. Everyone who is truly assimilated has something crucial they do for the organization. They are needed and they contribute in some significant way to the church winning in the community. Embrace the fact that service is essential to full integration into the church and design a method to get people serving. It is so good for everyone.

A good Service Strategy will do five things:
1. It will make serving opportunities known.
2. It will take recruiting seriously.
3. It will employ recognition strategies.
4. It will provide training, expectations, and guidelines for each position.
5. It will create significant serving opportunities for pre-Christians and pre-members.

As you go through each of these strategies, make a note of the things you are already doing at your church and which ones you should consider implementing.

Strategy #1: Make Serving Opportunities Known

If your church is actually going to assimilate people into the life of the church during the first year of their attendance, it is imperative that you offer multiple opportunities for people to get involved. It is important that visitors and attenders see the whole playing field and can survey all the various places where they might jump in and get involved.

It is important that the visitor not perceive that the church as a private club and somehow they are restricted from getting involved. Churches send this signal when they have no jobs for people who haven't joined the church yet, instead of clearly offering people opportunities to enjoy the wonder of service. Churches send this signal when membership is lifted high as the great goal to attain instead of proclaiming membership as one of the milestones on the road to a fully developed Christian life.

Churches send this signal when they talk about jobs, using lots of Christian slang instead of demystifying the service opportunity by talking in common everyday terms. Churches send this signal when only longtime members are approached for significant jobs instead of looking outside the box for new people to serve in various key roles. Churches send this kind of signal when it is assumed what is involved in a service assignment instead of going over it because someone may not know all about it. It is important that all kinds of jobs are presented as important, and not just teaching or babysitting jobs.

There are multiple opportunities to ask people to get involved and to get feedback about where people would like to get involved. Too many churches rely on the Sunday morning announcement time as their sole recruitment time. We will talk about other ways of recruiting people to get involved later, but take advantage of other opportunities to ask people to jump into involvement.

Every class is a chance to talk about the opportunities in the church to serve. Brochures that list specific opportunities for service are great ways of letting people know the details of a service opportunity. Preaching a whole sermon about service with actual service opportunities to sign up for at the end of the message is a great way to go beyond just announcements.

Early in the process of learning about the church, the value of service should be communicated. A special class on service should be included in the church orientation process.

Even in the visitor packets all the service opportunities can be handed out. Trained people in the lobby waiting to talk with folks about signing up for service opportunities sends a message of how much service is valued. This can be just one of the aspects of a good information booth.

It is crucial that everyone can see where and how they can pitch in right away. There will surely be jobs that a visitor cannot do, but they need to see what they can do and where they can get involved when they choose to get involved. Every ministry in the church should make a list of jobs that need doing in their area. These various lists should be compiled, regularly updated, and constantly distributed. When all the jobs at a church are known, it says "we are open to all kinds of people getting involved, not just the people who have deciphered the code and know the right people."

Some of the most effective churches at enlisting people into service put out brochures for every ministry opportunity in the church or in a specific department. Some churches include a brief description of each position so that people have an idea of what they are signing up for.

Below are two examples of church flyers and brochures that get all the opportunities to serve out in front of people so they can get involved. Too often we see churches that are almost secretive about the various jobs and opportunities in the church. It will help immensely if everybody understands what a fully staffed ministry program looks like.

One church created a brochure that lists all of the potential jobs that a person could do in this church. This was a tri-fold brochure that was made available to visitors, new members, and anyone interested in serving.

Places of Service

Administration
Church Administrator
Treasurer
Financial Secretary
Office Manager
Office Assistant
Youth Assistant
Children's Assistant
Worship Assistant

Assimilation
Assimilation Coordinator
Usher
Usher Ministry Coordinator
Greeter
Host/Hostess
Runner
Plant Ministry
Gift Drop Coordinator
Gift Drop Member
Auditorium Host
Info Booth Coordinator
Info Booth Member

Children's Ministry
Children's Coordinator
Children's As Coordinator
Nursery/Toddler Director
Nursery/Toddler worker
Primary Director (K-2)
Primary Teacher
Primary Teacher Assistant
Primary Helper
Middle Director (3-4)
Middle Teacher
Middle Teacher As
Middle Helper
Junior Director (5-6)
Junior Teacher
Junior Teacher As

Junior Helper
Pioneer Club Director
PC Games Director
PC Devotions Coordinator
PC worker
Kids Carnival Director
Child Care Provider

Community Impact
CI Coordinator
CI Members

Compassion
Compassion Coordinator
Food Bank Coordinator
Food Bank Worker
Clothes Closet Coordinator
Clothes Closet Worker
Prison Ministry Member
Widow Ministry Member
Substance Abuse Ministry
Elderly Ministry
Grieving Ministry
Divorce Ministry
Mentoring Moms Ministry

Discipleship
University of Life Dean
Home Group Leader
Home Group Assistant
Bible Study Leader
Bible Study Teacher

Drama
Drama Coordinator
Drama Team Member

Evangelism
Evangelism Coordinator
Evangelism Team Member
Newborn Ministry
Newly Married Ministry

Library
Librarian
Assistant Librarian

Maintenance
Maintenance Coordinator
Landscape Coordinator
Landscape Member
Set-up/Tear-down Leader
Set-up/Tear-down Crew
Planning Team Member

Men's Ministry
Men's Ministry Coordinator
Men's Ministry Leader
Men's Breakfast Coordinator
Men's Breakfast Team Member
Men's Retreat Coordinator
Men's Retreat Member

Mission
Missions Coordinator
Missions Team Member

Music
Children's Choir Coordinator
Children's Choir Support Staff
Worship Pastor
Worship Team Leader
Worship Team Member
Sound and Lighting Technician
Special Music Minister

Prayer
Prayer Ministry Coordinator
Prayer Cell Leader
Prayer Cell Member

Publications
Publications Director
Newsletter Coordinator
Sermon Ministry Coordinator
Sermon Ministry Team Member
Advertising Coordinator
Advertising Team Member
Photography

Recovery
Recovery Coordinator
Alcohol Recovery Leader
Alcohol Recovery As
Drug Recovery Leader
Drug Recovery As
Lust Recovery Leader
Lust Recovery Assistant
Virtues Recovery Leader
Virtues Recovery Assistant
Domestic Violence Recovery Leader
Domestic Violence Recovery Assistant

Retreats Coordinator
Men's
Women's
Children's
Couples
Singles
Leaders

Singles
Singles Ministry Leader
Singles Ministry Assistant

Women's
Women's Ministry Coordinator
Women's Team Member
Single Mom's Leader
Crafts Director
Women's Group Leader

Youth
Youth Pastor
Youth Ministry Coordinator
High School Youth Director
High School Youth Assistant
Jr High Leader
Jr High Assistant

I am ready to serve in: _____

I would like to be contacted about:

_____

Name:

Phone:

E.C.A.M.
(Every Christian A Minister)

> *"For the equipping of the saints for the work of service, to the building up of the body of Christ."*
> EPHESIANS 4:12

You will not fully experience the joy of the Christian life until you are involved in serving our Lord in a regular ministry. If you are not involved, look and pray through the opportunities. There is a place of ministry for you.

Prayerfully consider one of these areas:

Worship & Creative Arts

Junior Choir
  Director

Instrumentalists:
  Brass
  Woodwinds
  Strings

Saturday Night
  Piano/Keyboard Players
  Vocalists
  Bass Players
  Drummers
  Electric & Acoustic Guitarists

Sunday Night
  Vocalists
  Bass Players
  Drummers
  Electric & Acoustic Guitarists

Technical Ministries
  Saturday
    Multimedia Operators

  Sunday
    Audio Assistants
    Audio Console Operators
    Lighting Console Operators
    House Directors

(No experience necessary, training will be provided.)

Children's Ministries

Sunday 9:00am or 10:45am
  Nursery/Toddlers
  2s, 3s, 4s, 5s
  Kindergarten

Primary Department (grades 1-3)
Junior Department (grades 4-5
Sunday Support Staff

Saturday Night
  Nursery / Toddler
  2s, 3s, 4s – Jr Kids
  Grades 2-5 – Kids Church

Service / Caring

Caring Corps
  Home Repairs
  Transportation
  Food Preparations
  Food Servers
  Automotive Repair

VIPS
  Visit Homebound
  Visit Assisted Care Facilities

Front Door Ministries
  Ushers
  Greeters
  Prayer Team

Welcome Table
   Host or Hostess
   Coffee Servers

Library
   Coordinator
   Assistants
   Database/Catalogue Assistant

Academy & Preschool
   Prayer for the ministry impact of the school in the lives of our students and their families

   Help supervising students at play during lunch and recess

   Parking lot assistance during special events

Women's Ministries

MOM's Committee
   Table Leaders
   Decorations
   Child Care
   (2 hours – once a month)
   CD Ministry

Bible Study Team
   Greeters
   Computer input
   Children's Teachers
   Helpers for luncheons

Student Ministries

Rock and Flock
   Small group leaders
   Teachers
     Sunday Morning
     Tuesday/Thursday Evening
   Event Staff
   Audio, lighting, multimedia
     Sunday Morning
     Tuesday/Thursday Evening

SERVICE STRATEGY

Worship Musicians
Chaperones
Drivers

Life Stage Ministries
Leadership
Class Leader
Assimilation
Caring

Men's Ministry

Senior Adult Ministry
Assist with Events

Bible Breakfasts
Cooks
Coordinators

When you have marked the areas you are interested in serving, you may place this form in the offering basket, hand to an usher at the close of the service, or drop off / mail to the church office.

Name(s): _____

Phone: _____

Email: _____

I am currently involved in the following ministry:

_____

_____

Strategy #2: Take Recruitment Seriously

It would be wonderful if all new people were like Pete and Samantha at the beginning of this chapter, but they are not. In fact, most will not get involved until they are asked. Remember this truth: MOST PEOPLE WILL NOT GET INVOLVED UNLESS THEY ARE ASKED. Telling people from the pulpit about a crisis is not considered asking by most people. There have been surveys taken that suggest between forty to sixty percent of the people in a church will not get involved unless they are specifically and personally asked by someone they respect in the church. There are five generally accepted methods for recruiting people into service assignments in the church.

1. Pulpit Announcements

The first method for recruiting people into service in the church is through the announcements during the main worship service. This method has been used and abused for centuries. It tends to work in churches with under a hundred people, and it has an increasing lack of success in churches that are larger. When a church has under a hundred people, the person who is making the announcements is usually an influencer in the congregation and they know who should probably respond to this kind of announcement. The announcement time can also be a time of great guilt because there is just no one else to respond.

So, in many way announcements in a small church is like personal recruitment but is easier on the recruiter. This is why announcements in this kind of church are effective. While every church must have and make announcements, realize that it should not be relied upon to raise up volunteers.

2. Personal Recruitment

The second method for raising up volunteers and getting people involved in the church life is personal recruitment. This is practically the gold standard for recruitment and every pastor and lay leader who wants to head up a thriving ministry needs to develop good skills in personal recruitment, or their ministry will be held back. Jesus said, "Ask and you shall receive." It is true when it comes to recruiting people to get involved. The pastor and any lay leader of a ministry must constantly spend time calling people on the phone to recruit them for ministry assignments. I usually suggest that a pastor of a church under a thousand must spend a minimum of two hours per week personally recruiting people.

Personal recruitment seems to work best if it is a five-step process. First, start with prayer for the position or for the new person in the congregation. "Lord, what do want Bill and Mary Johnson to be doing for you here in the church?" "Lord, we need three Children's Church workers for the story time; please lead me to the people who can do this crucial function."

Second, look at the directory of names in the church including new visitors and attenders and/or look at the list of jobs that are available in the church. Allow the Lord in prayer to match up or highlight who goes with which job.

Third, call the person on the phone and tell them about your time of prayer: "Bill, this is Pastor Jim at First Church. I was just praying for you and your family, and as I prayed it seemed that God put you on my heart as someone who could get involved in men's ministry helping out with the breakfasts. I don't want you to tell me whether you will do it or not because if I asked you right now, you would probably say no. But I would like to ask you if you would pray about it for a couple of days and ask God if He wants you to do it." "If he says 'no,' then I am certainly okay with that, and we can find another place to get you involved." "If he says, 'yes,' then let's get you trained in that ministry and get you involved." "Will you pray for the next couple of days about this ministry?"

Fourth, follow up with Bill to find out how the prayer time went. If he prayed about the opportunity and God prompted him to get involved, then introduce him to the men's ministry coordinator and get him trained. If he prayed about that opportunity and felt that God did not want him to do that ministry, then move to the fifth part of personal recruitment.

Fifth, ask Bill what he thinks his gifts, interests, and/or skills are that he could offer back to the Lord as an offering. It is important that you approach Bill with the mindset that he will be supremely benefited by getting involved. You are not asking Bill for a favor. Instead you are asking Bill to release his gifts to the Lord, to please the Lord, to build up treasure in heaven, to change people's lives, to help the community, etc. You are doing Bill a favor by pulling him into service for the Lord. As you listen to him more closely, it will become obvious where Bill needs to serve the Lord. Even if it is a temporary assignment, it will become clear where God would have him serve. Remember that non-service is not an option. He needs to serve somewhere.

3. Automatic Sign-Ups, Mandatory Participation

The third option for having more people involved in service in the church is automatic sign-ups. This is somewhat controversial and some churches will not use this method. Let me explain how I realized the power of automatic sign-ups. I was talking with the children's director of a church of about 125 people, and she asked me if I would pray for her as she was going to have an extremely busy week this next week because she had too many people signing up to help in children's ministry. I paused and asked her to repeat what she just said. "You have too many people signing up for children's ministry?!" "Yes," she said, "I need prayer because I have to be out every night this week training all these people." "Nobody has this problem!" I exclaimed, "What are you doing in your ministry that is causing too many people to sign up to help?"

She then went on to explain the process of automatic sign-ups. I have since heard of other churches that use this process for a number of their ministries. Even some public schools and sports teams use this process to get volunteers for their organizations. Automatic sign-ups usually work like this. If a parent puts their child or teen into the child care area or the youth group, then they are given a form that they have to fill out as to where they want to serve in that ministry. It is required that the person serve at least two hours a month, but they could serve up to ten hours per week. This young lady had printed a list of all the jobs in the children's ministry with an estimation of the amount of hours it would take to do the job. Every person who put their child into children's ministry needed to sign up for one of the jobs. Once the job was filled, then it was crossed off and the list of available jobs was less. She trained all those who "signed up" so that they would understand how the children's ministry was done in that church.

Some churches will not use this method because they want people who want to serve and do not want a person to feel forced to be involved. Some churches feel that this method is too dictatorial and heavy-handed and gives the church a bad name. You and your church must make the decision about whether you use this method; but I do know that if used well with pleasant people, it is a surefire way to get people involved and have a first class amount of people helping out. In an age of less and less automatic willingness to serve, automatic sign-ups can help. Some churches have put an opt-out clause in the sign-ups for those who are already serving in other areas of the church.

One of the true benefits that this automatic sign-up method does achieve is that it gets newcomers involved right away. Most churches have a three-week waiting period before you are contacted about your automatic responsibilities in the nursery or children's ministry if you put your children there. New people can complain about it, but it gets them over the initial hump and connects them to the other people with whom they are serving.

4. Ministry Fair
The fourth option for getting people involved in church service is by having a ministry fair. This is where the whole church

worship service is about serving the Lord. The singing and sermon is directed toward one goal: having people sign up to check out various opportunities to serve in and through the church. The sermon is usually shorted and pointed toward the various opportunities that are available at church and/or spiritual gifts are taught with their deployment being encouraged. The highlight of this kind of service is that booths or tables have been placed at the back of the church, in the lobby, or out on the patio representing every ministry in the church. Each individual can get up and take the time to talk to different ministries that they might be interested in. Every booth and/or table has a sign-up sheet for people to put down their contact information. This allows people to seek out the areas that they would like to explore with the Lord.

As a church gets larger, this "Ministry Fair" Sunday becomes an essential part of raising up volunteers for the ministries of the church. I talked with one youth pastor in a very large church of 7,000, who said that all they do is use the list of people who sign up at the ministry fair. They have training designed to get these new folks up to speed with what is happening in their ministry, but this is where they find the people who are interested in their ministry. This is a way to make sure that people do not fall through the cracks. It allows people to feel included by being given a chance to jump into various ministries they might not have known about because they do not know anyone in those ministries.

Many larger churches have found this to be a wonderful boon to their ministry, but smaller churches and medium-sized churches have not been as successful with the ministry fair model. The smaller church and the medium-sized church must rely on personal recruitment and even pulpit announcements for new volunteers.

5. Service Classes

The fifth way of getting people to jump into serving the Lord is through classes that identify gifts, passions, abilities, and experiences. Many churches now have these classes that help people understand where they will function best in the church. These classes can be especially helpful in identifying people who have particular gifts and getting them plugged into the right ministry for them. These classes also send the message to the people in the church that we are here for you. We want you to serve where you will be maximally effective.

These classes are the most effective at helping people understand their "want to" ministry area. Every person has two kinds of ministry that they need to do in a church: "have to" and "want to." "Have to" ministries are those areas of ministry that have to be done and there is no one else to do it. Every person has had to serve in a "have to" ministry for a period of time. "Want to" ministry are those kinds of ministry that fit who you are as a person, and it provides you with a level of encouragement and joy that you want to just keep doing it even if no one ever compliments you or notices you.

These classes also help people identify why they didn't particularly enjoy a particular "have to" assignment. They help narrow down where a "want to" assignment might be for them. These classes can be short, introductory classes and/or long, detailed personal exploratory classes. Both kinds of classes are helpful but for the purposes of visitor assimilation, the short class is better for visitors so that they can get involved in the first year.

Strategy #3: Employ Recognition Strategies
The people who set up and serve the Lord by using their time, gifts, and desires are heroes in the church. Too often in the church the pastor is the hero and the lay people are all there just to support him. You must turn this around and celebrate, congratulate, and appreciate the people who volunteer to serve the Lord. Most churches do a lousy job of celebrating their wins. The reason why churches can forget to celebrate is because even if you have a great service, there is another service next week.

A church that draws people into service is constantly encouraging and appreciating the people who volunteer. It is very helpful if each area of ministry just thinks about what they are going to celebrate as a regular part of ministry. It could take place every quarter at the very least. If the church gets larger with lots of varied sub-ministries, this may move to once a month.

There are three ways of giving appreciation and praise. There is spoken praise, where a group or team or individual is praised directly, indirectly, or in front of a group for something they have achieved. This is very powerful and should be done much more often. Many people never hear any verbal praise from their work, their home, or their friends. So to be praised for their service to the Lord is very enriching and encouraging. There is also written praise, where a group, team, or an individual is given a letter or note praising them for their work in a certain project. In many ways this is more powerful than verbal because people can go back and read and re-read the note that says that they are valuable and doing good things.

I know of people who have posted note cards of praise in their office cubicle. I know of people who have framed letters of praise and appreciation and put it on their wall at home. The third way to praise a person for their contribution to the church is through a tangible object. This can be a plaque or a ring or a dinner out or some other actual physical thing that says that we really appreciate what you have done for us. I believe that more churches need to get better at inventing and giving out tangible gifts of appreciation to the people who make the church go forward.

All of these ways of celebrating and rewarding and giving appreciation keep saying that this church is a place where you can get involved and you want to get involved. This sends a powerful message to the visitors and encourages their desire to assimilate into this church.

Strategy #4: Provide Training, Expectations, and Guidelines for each Position
Too often in church work we recruit people to a job that they have to invent themselves. They get little or no feedback as to whether they are doing a good job or not, and they are never relieved of or given time off. I have noticed that the churches that succeed at recruiting volunteers often have more clear

instructions for the volunteers before they take the assignment. Sometimes this means a full job description. I have preferred reducing every assignment down to four to eight specific things that are crucial for success in that assignment. This lets people know what they have to do to please the person who recruited them. We all want to do a good job and get praise and appreciation. This ensures that will happen.

Below are examples of some of the success steps that we made for each position in the church so that we could have people jump in and be successful more quickly.

7 Actions of a Good Usher

Smile.
Look people in the eye.
Extend a bulletin.
Say "Hello, Welcome to (Church Name)!"
Offer to find them a seat; "May I find you a seat?"
Tell parents with small children that there is a nursery and offer to escort them.
During Service, immediately approach a mother with a fussy baby and suggest that she go to the nursery.

4 Keys of a Good Hospital Visit

A Look: Make good eye contact with the person and ask them questions.
A Word: Open the Bible, read it out loud, and give them a word of encouragement.
A Touch: Hold their hand or arm, especially when

you pray.

A Prayer: Pray for them...Listen what God would have you pray.

5 Actions of a Good Greeter

Smile.
Say "Hello!"
Offer your name first.
Extend your hand.
Ask F.O.R. questions:
- *Family:* Is this your family?
  Do you live around here?
- *Occupation:* What do you do for a living?
- *Religion*: How long have you been worshipping at (Church Name)?

7 Actions of an Information Host

Smile.
Look people in the eye.
Say "Hello, May I help you?"
Listen intently until the person finishes talking.
Answer their questions thoroughly.
Ask them to fill out a guest card: "I would be happy to escort you to that location. Would you please fill out this guest card first?"
Offer them coffee and/or donuts.

5 Actions of a Good Guest Visit
Knock or rring the door bell clearly.
Smile.
Say, "Hello, we are from (Church Name).
We just wanted to say thank you for stopping by our church today…"
Hand them the gift: Do not stay more than 5 minutes.
If they are not home…leave the gift with a handwritten note that says, "Thanks for visiting with us at _____."

7 Weekly Actions of a Great Sunday School Teacher
Practice daily time of Bible study and prayer.
Pray for the members of your class.
Evangelize the members of your class.
Prepare an interactive lesson for Sunday.
Write or phone the members of your class.
Reward those who bring a friend, their Bible, and an obedient spirit.
Attend Church.

Strategy #5: Consider Significant Jobs for Pre-Christians and Pre-Members

Many churches do not realize that they are restricting people from getting involved in the church by only offering the "bad jobs" to the newcomers. If all the good and desirable jobs are taken, and only the difficult, mundane, or routinized jobs are available, then we are saying to people that we do not really want them to be a part of our church; we just want them to be our servants.

New people feel included when they are actually included in the crucial functions of the life of the church. In order for new people to feel that they are a part of the church, there must be jobs that they can do, even for those who have not yet committed to the faith. This is difficult for some churches to embrace, but not every job requires that a person be a believer in Jesus Christ. Now some jobs certainly require an embrace of the faith, but not all jobs. Those people who are on their way to saving faith may want to get involved as they are feeling the drawing love of the Savior. In every area of ministry there are these jobs that pre-Christians and pre-members can do. A church should have a clear-cut policy on how they will handle this situation. If there are no jobs for those who are in the process of deciding to become members, then the church becomes a private club with MEMBERS ONLY signs up everywhere.

I am often asked what kinds of jobs pre-Christians and pre-members could do. They might be invited to sing in a choir or to help chaperone a youth event. They might be asked to give their expertise on a particular decision the church is facing. They might be asked to drive for youth trips. They might be asked to bring their perspective to the assimilation process of the church. They might be asked to be inviters to the church as they probably have the most friends who don't go to the church. They might be asked to make costumes or help throw a banquet or party. They might be asked to help feed the homeless or work at the homeless shelter. There are all kinds of services that they can perform to the Lord that does not require that they have already made a profession of faith or have already become members.

I realize that there are churches that use membership as a restrictor to involvement so that people will sign up to be members. While I do not recommend this method, this is one way of using membership. Even churches that do not allow members to do much usually do not require that the electrician who works on the air conditioning system be a member of the church. They usually do not require that the real estate agent that they use to find a new home for the pastor be a member. The list can go on and on. Churches delegate responsibilities to non-members and non-Christians all the time, and we should have a clear policy as to how that will work for your church.

In some churches, the line requiring membership is clearly at teaching and holding office in the church. In some churches you can teach one semester as a non-member if you have shared your testimony and the leadership has accepted your profession of faith. There are all kinds of jobs that would be able to be performed with or without referring to the faith. These jobs could be opened up to those who are a part of the church but have not committed to membership yet. There do need to be a few strategies put into place to ensure the pre-Christians and pre-members succeed in their jobs.

1. **Increase monitoring and mentoring.**
When a church embraces the idea of getting new people involved in service, they need to make sure that the assignment turns

out positive. This means that the people in the church need to manage the person and see if this opportunity really fits them. This is where those who recruited the person should ask, "How did it go when you served in that ministry?" "How could your experience have been improved?" The person who served should have been observed and then told at least one thing they did right in their service. There should be a big emphasis on what they did right.

Reasonable management and mentoring is what people expect if they go outside of their comfort zone and volunteer for something that they do not have a high level of expertise in. The church has in the past been woefully inadequate in this regard. We have had more of a "throw you in the deep end of the pool mindset." "If you make it to the side of the pool, then we will keep you and throw you in again next week." There is also an implicit idea by most people that, "If I am willing to volunteer at this church, I will receive a higher level of mentoring than the person who does not volunteer." This implicit idea is often shattered on the rocks of reality after two years of service for the church. Work hard at mentoring the people who step forward to make the church operate effectively.

I realize that there is the nagging desire to reach out to new people, but those who are being assimilated need to be given special care. A general rule of thumb that I use for staff and volunteers is: Those who serve full-time should receive an hour a week of mentoring. Those who serve part-time (10-30 hours a week) should receive an hour every other week of mentoring. Those who serve less than ten hours per week should be invited to an hour a month or an hour a quarter mentoring time so they can be valued and developed.

2. Allow and encourage movement across ministry lines.

If a church commits itself to assimilating people, then it must move new people into service. If it moves new people into service, there will be mismatches, which will have to be fixed. This is not a bad thing; it is a good thing. Most people have to go through three to five "have to" ministries before they settle on a "want to" that they will do the rest of their ministry lives. This means that a church must be open to movement across ministry lines, movement across category boundaries, and movement across issues. The church must encourage and celebrate when a person finds that they do not fit in one ministry and wants to try another ministry. In fact, the pastor must often give cover fire for a person to switch ministries.

One idea that is quite successful is to initiate a "First Serve" program. This is a trial run or apprentice position. Many people would like to take a ministry for a test drive for a week or so if they had a chance to observe and be trained. More and more churches are using this title "First Serve" as a way to take the pressure off of people's serving interest. They will openly tell people that this is just a trial run and they can see if it is for them or not.

3. Watch out for weary volunteers or mismatches.

We also need to train our leaders to be observant of volunteers who aren't fitting in to their roles, or are getting weary. I can remember saying to lots of people who looked like they were getting weary in a particular ministry, "I have been praying for you and I have been thinking that you might fit in this other ministry. Would you pray about that?" This offers people the ability to say that the pastor asked if I would think about this other ministry. It is the ministry leader's job to notice when a person, even the leader, is losing steam and not enjoying their service.

In some smaller churches people have to die to be able to legitimately move to another area of ministry. If your church sees Sally or Ben or Molly not as individual Christians but as the director of a particular program, then it is extremely difficult to allow them to step out of that program. This can be deadly. New people bring new ideas and new energy to the whole of a church. Let people move across ministry lines and you will be surprised at how many people will have a new energy for serving the Lord because they are serving in a new area.

SERVICE STRATEGY

What will your church do to get people participating in serving the Lord and His church?

	Needed	Cost	Time	Approval	Person
First Serve					
Ministry Fair					
Brochures					
Recovery SG					
Training					
Recruiting					
Opportunities Presented					
Rewards					
Success Steps					
Seeker Responsibilities					
Monitoring Mentoring					

Chapter 8

Friendship Strategy

Rose and Henry were new to the area and wanted to get to know people in their new community, so they began going to churches. They were not looking for God; they were looking for couples like themselves with whom to be friends. They attended a number of churches over the first six months they lived in town, but most churches just left it up to the visitors to get to know people in the church. It was not their business to help people make friends. It was the church's business to help people to connect with God. Henry and Rose kept searching by going to different churches until they came to First Church. It was very warm and friendly and before they knew it, they had made three friends in First Church. The pastor was not the best speaker that they had heard, but they had found what they were looking for—friends. First Church had a plan for helping couples like Rose and Henry make friends. It is why they stayed at First Church and why they eventually trusted Christ as their Savior at First Church. First Church met their need for friendship and then introduced them to God.

It has been suggested that over 80% of the people who visit a church are looking for friendships. They will add a relationship with God if a church meets the need they feel for new friendships. Too many churches leave it up to the visitors to make friends on their own. This is a very difficult road to travel for a new person. Churches that are constantly gaining new people are those churches that connect new people with others so that lasting relationships spring up. There are a number of actions that an organized church can take that will increase the connections between people. Not everyone will be able to connect at even a great connecting church, but many more will if you sit down and create a simple plan.

A good friendship strategy does three specific things: it creates an environment that is conducive to friendship; it encourages the actions that create friendships; it removes barriers that prevent friendships. Here are some things to consider when creating a friendship environment.

1. Group Size—Small Enough to Connect
One of the first rules for creating a friendship environment is to foster group environments that are conducive to developing friendships. Groups must be small enough for a person to connect with individuals in that group. This "small enough" size is different in various generations and cultures, but there is a discernable number that is too large.

In the recent past, a Sunday School class of between forty to one hundred was the right size for making friendships. The current generation in America finds anything over about fifteen is not conducive to making friends. This means that small groups are more popular and more of them are needed.

2. Physical Arrangement of the Room

A second issue for creating a friendship environment is that the physical arrangement of the room and people will help create friends or take away from friendship creation. A lecture format with people facing the back of each other's heads is not going to work to help create friends in this current climate. In order to make friends, two people have to see each other and watch them to see if they are interested in being friends with that person. So a big circle with everyone being able to view everyone else helps this pre-friendship observation.

> *Friendships don't just happen. They need to be nurtured & grown in the right kind of environment.*

3. Sufficient Pool of Potential Friends

A third issue is having enough people for a person to potentially become friends with. This does not mean that there must be a lot of people; it means that there must be a sufficient number of people of the type and interests that people are searching for in their friends. This means that a church must often have large gatherings that draw in more people from a particular age or life-stage. It also means that at times it is important to gather all the ladies who are serving in various parts of the church so that new ladies can see all the potential people with whom to connect.

4. Remembering Names

A fourth issue for friendship creation is learning and remembering people's name. If a person forgets another person's name, they feel embarrassed to ask a second time and often will avoid the person that they would really like to become friends with because they can't remember their name. A few churches have created a whole new climate in their church by having everyone in the church wear a disposable nametag every Sunday. This eliminates this barrier and has electrified the amount of connections between people. Another way that churches have dealt with this barrier is to put people into small groups below fourteen people. For some reason, if there are more than fourteen people in a group, then people, especially men, seem to believe that they do not have to remember people's names. It can also be very helpful if the leader says the name of each person a few times during every meeting.

5. Create Affinity and Common Interest Groups

A fifth issue that is needed for friendship creation is affinity and/or common interests. Friendships must have a common interest that can be shared by both friends. Someone's family problems are not a common interest that a healthy friendship can be built around. Both people in a friendship must enjoy a common interest so that their interest in that thing will draw them together. Then the exchange of personal information, feelings, plans, etc., cements the friendships. This means that a church must have a number of ways to connect with people. These may be any number of different activities and interests. More and more churches are realizing that offering Bible studies as the only friendship-building small group limits the amount of people who can connect over that interest. Some churches are expanding their small group offerings to any interest of people in the congregation. This seems to work especially well for churches that use a sermon-based small group format as people can discuss and apply the sermon around and over all kinds of activities and interests. People want to find other people who like to do what they like to do. After this affinity is exposed, then the spiritual elements can be explored and deepened. Remember, people may not let you introduce them to the friendship of God until they make human friends with people in your congregation.

6. Allow for Deeper, Personal Sharing Opportunities

A sixth issue that is needed for friendship creation is sharing deeper, more personal material. If people are to move past just sharing the same church building and pastor, they need to be given a forum where they can share deeper material from their life. It is amazing how much energy is released when a real person that they know shares a testimony of how God has dealt with them or is dealing with them.

These glimpses into the soul of the person are what allow a friendship to go the next level. This is why small groups give everyone in the group the opportunity to share a prayer request that everyone in the group will write down and pray for at least once in the coming week. People are then free to share at whatever depth they feel comfortable. More and more churches are bringing back testimonies in the main service. Some churches call these faith stories and make videos of people's deeply moving encounters with God or prayer requests being answered or miracle accounts. There is a hunger to go beneath the surface with others. There must be adequate time and vehicles in the smaller groups to let this happen. If there is too much lecture or other material in each class or group, then friendship potential is killed. The church can so easily help people open up with others by asking everyone to share.

7. Work With, Talk With, Play With

A seventh issue that helps create the matrix for friendship is realizing that relationships improve in only three ways: work with, talk with, play with. The significance should be placed on the "with" component. There are some friendships that will never form or never go the next level until two people work with each other. There are some friendships that will never go to the next level until two people sit down and have an honest or deeper conversation with each other. There are some friendships that will never blossom fully until two people play together. If the church is interested in this dynamic area of friendship, then it will see to it that these essential vehicles for taking friendships deeper take place.

I know of churches that put people in teams for serving in the church as a way to help people work together. There are churches that help people participate in compassion work projects, which always bonds those who participate. There are churches that decrease the teaching time and increase the talking time in their small groups out of a desperate need for hearing from others in their own words.

8. Ask Free-Flowing Questions

An eighth critical issue for creating a climate in which friendships can flourish is to encourage free flowing questions. This involves providing questions that people can ask each other. These questions would go beneath the surface and would allow the other person to reveal something about themselves that they might not have shared up to that point. Questions can be intimidating so many people never get around to asking them of the people that they would like to be friends with. A friendship does not deepen and grow unless questions are asked and answered.

When a church or small group provides an environment in which deep, interesting questions are asked frequently, this provides a rich soil in which friendships can grow and develop. Some churches have pre-printed questions about topics related to the sermon that allow a person to reveal things about their life, family, and dreams. Some churches have a sharing time in which "What do you think?" questions are asked and answered. Too often churches are completely solution-oriented and Bible-knowledge driven and thereby have not allowed people to reveal who they are to other people in their small group.

Friendship Environment Quick Reference Table

Friendship Environment Issue	Example
Small enough group to connect	
Physical arrangement of the room	
Pool of potential friends	
Remembering names	
Common interests, affinities	
Deeper personal material	
Work with, talk with, play with	
Free-flowing questions	

What will your church do to help people make friends?

A good friendship strategy involves the constant maintenance of programs, groups, and/or meetings that connect people to the church and each other, as well as remove any barriers that inhibit friendship. There are eight different kinds of programs that work especially well. Not every church needs to run these all the time, but over the course of a year a church that wants to retain its visitors will do these various programs. The larger that a church has become, the more it will be running these programs all the time. These break down the impersonal nature of a larger church into a place where people can find connection and friendships. Do not be overwhelmed by this list, especially if your church is not doing many of these programs, groups, or meetings. Digest this information and look at starting these ideas over the course of a year or two in a phased way as to allow the church to catch up to where it can be in terms of friendship and friendliness.

1. Newcomer's Dessert

The first thing that a church must look at inserting into its regular church calendar is a Newcomer's Dessert usually at the pastor's home. When a church is small this may not need to take place more than once a quarter. As the church would grow and more people would visit, then it may need to take place more frequently. I know of a church of over **6,000** in which the pastor still has the Newcomer's Dessert in his home once a month to get to know the new people to the church.

This Newcomer's Dessert is an informal gathering for people to get to know the pastor, key staff, and volunteers. Usually it is not possible to put more than twenty people in a living room, so this makes a good cut-off point. Everyone is seated on the couches and the pastor opens in prayer and then asks each person to briefly share their name and how they heard about or started coming to the church. This allows everyone, including the pastor, to talk about the same thing and be on an equal footing. Even the pastor shares how he came to the church and where he was before he came.

Then the pastor will usually share a broad statement about the vision or values of the church and allow each of the staff people or volunteers present to briefly share about their ministry. This gives the newcomers to the church a larger vision of the church. It also usually sparks questions from those who have come. As you allow questions, it engages a number of the people who really did want to dig into understanding the church at a new level.

Dessert is next and creates an opportunity for people to eat and seek out other people that they would like to talk with. Gathering in the kitchen for a quick prayer and then allowing people to pick the pie, cookies, or cake that they would like, brings a new level of conversation and interaction. Sometimes a person finds another person who is new to the church to talk with. Sometimes people seek out a staff member or particular ministry volunteer. Sometimes people seek out the pastor. But the amount of mixing and interaction is significant to bonding with this new church.

2. Encourage Small Gestures of Inclusion — lunch invitations, assigning a buddy, sub-ministries

A second constant program that often is overlooked is small gestures of inclusion. Keep telling people from the pulpit to invite people to lunch and not just to go out with their friends. One elder in a church had a brilliant strategy for turning the church into a friendly place. He would stand up during the announcement time and tell all the visitors that he was so glad that they had come to the church. He hoped that they would not be too overwhelmed by the number of people who invited them out to lunch following the service but the people at the church just liked to include new people.

He said this same kind of thing week after week after week, until it was expected that people would overwhelm the visitors with invitations to lunch. The church grew from around eighty to over three hundred in just a few years with this kind of friendliness approach.

One church assigned people to be on call each Sunday to take people out to lunch. These were usually people who went to lunch anyway almost every Sunday. The pastor had previously arranged with these couples that if he introduced new people to these couples on call, that was the signal for the couple in the church to ask this new couple out to lunch. This was a way to insure that some of the best and most engaging couples were taking the new people out to lunch. This gave the new couple access to more information about the church but also connected them to couples that they might fit with more naturally. Sometimes the people who invite others to lunch with a blanket call are those who can never get people who know them to go to lunch with them.

One church that was in a declining area, population-wise, saw visitors as so valuable that a buddy was assigned to each visitor so that the highest possible retention rate of visitors took place. This buddy, who was assigned to the visitors during staff meetings or before, called the person during the week. They offered to pray for the person and answer any of the questions the person might have about the church. They offered to sit with the visitor the next Sunday. They also offered to pick the person up and bring them to church if they did not have a ride. This strategy allowed the church to intensively love on the visitors because visitors are the life of the church in the future. This was especially true for this church in an area of declining population.

Many times it is not the church service itself that really connects a person to the church as much as a particular sub-ministry and the people in that ministry. The more exposure that a person can have to the various sub-ministries in a church, the better chance they have of connecting and staying at the church. This means that the children's ministry people may need to do the welcoming of new visitors in the service. It may mean that the youth pastor may need to be up front more during the service so parents and teens can connect with him. It may mean that the visitation or care pastor may need to be much more visible so that the visitor in need can connect with this person and be more open when they share a need. There are dozens of smaller sub-ministries from Women's to

Recovery to Men's to Ushering, and it is these people who will ultimately connect the visitor to the church. Give them a bigger role in welcoming and it will pay off.

3. Church Orientation Program

A third program that needs to be maintained is the church orientation program. This needs massive amounts of energy, but it is well worth it. We have spent considerable time in this book talking about this crucial program. But let me say again that new people do not know how to connect to your church unless you show them. Step by step, you can help them warm up to the values, commitments, and people of your church.

This cannot be left to chance. Have a series of short classes where people can learn and get to know others who just came to the church. Have each person write out a nametag every week so that everyone can remember everyone's name. Make a new class if there are going to be more than twelve people in the class. This allows everyone to sense that they need to remember the people in the class as individuals and not just parts of this collective whole. Have people sit around one big table instead of creating rows, which makes the class lecture format less conducive to people connections.

The class leader should stop the class with at least fifteen minutes left in the class and ask every person for a prayer request from each person. "How may we pray for you this week?" "Do you have a prayer request you would like to share with us this week?" These times of sharing what people would like to be prayed for can be the highlight of the whole class. It is also wonderful that the next week people can come and share how God answered the prayer request from the previous week.

Remember that orienting people to the church is crucial, but that one of the key components of the orientation is orienting people to the other people who make up the church. If a church is successful at communicating all the information and values of the organization but there are no people connections, then the church orientation has been a failure because the people are the church. No one wants to join an organization; they want to work with people they like to accomplish a common cause or goal.

4. Small Group Life — for life transformation and community development

The fourth area of an effective Friendship Strategy is to have a vibrant small group life. While it is wonderful and powerful to have dynamic worship experiences where hundreds of people feel the power of praise and teaching in a large group, it is usually the dynamism and vibrancy of small groups that truly brings about life transformation. We as humans are social creatures, and we need social connection to be at our best. When small group ministries are what they should be, then care, compassion, evangelism, shepherding, teaching, and fun all take place with people you know. I used to tell people in the church I served that if they only came to the worship services and did not get involved in the small group life of the church, that within two years they would drop out of this church and stop attending. We saw this happen so much over my years as a pastor. People who loved the worship service and loved the teaching from the pulpit, but did not get involved in the next level of discipleship, would eventually drift off and do something else with their life. In order to really make a lasting connection with a church, one needs to plug into Sunday School or Home Studies or Men's groups, etc., some form of small group life that ministers to them at their stage of life.

New people need to have a sense that they are starting something new along with everybody else. Therefore many churches have adopted the plan of having their small groups start in September and run for six to twelve weeks and then end right before Christmas. Then a whole new group will start the first few weeks of January and run for six to twelve weeks and then come to an end. Another new group will start around the first of April or right after Easter and run for six to twelve weeks. Many churches have small groups take the summer off or only run a few small groups. Even though the teachers may be the same, they are teaching different curriculum and this allows new people to come to the class with a fresh start as everybody else. If a new person comes to a class that has been going for years and everybody knows everybody, then they can feel like an outsider and less welcomed.

There are various forms that small-group life can take; the variation must be present to pull all the people in the church into it. There are at least six different kinds of small-group life that can go on in a church. Not all of these will be happening in each church, but as the church grows, these various expressions of small-group life will begin springing up. There are those groups that are largely content driven, where 80% of the group time is taken up with hearing new material. There are fellowship groups that spend 70-80% of the group's time talking and discussing. It could be the pastor's sermon that is discussed or some other curriculum; the significant thing is that the members do most of the talking rather than a teacher. There are ministry groups where 70-80% of the time in the group is spent ministering to some need. There are affinity groups where 70-80% of the time in the group is spent doing something that everyone in the group finds interesting, like stitching or kayaking or running or whatever.

Some churches have been slow to embrace these kinds of groups; but as long as there is prayer and some devotional, it can allow Christians to connect and develop deep friendships around their mutual interests. There are recovery groups where people get the chance to apply Christian solutions to the specific issues that are really causing damage in their life. There are leadership groups where people are drawn together by the desire to be a next-level Christian leader. Each of these kinds of small-group life is valid and vital to a thriving church. The content small group has dominated church life for a long time, but more and more churches are realizing that just more Bible information does not bring about biblical transformation.

5. Friendship Training—listening skills, required ingredients, levels of friendship

More and more people are coming to realize that they do not know how to make friends. This is true in every area of life. People don't know how to make friends with their spouse and so they increasingly drift away from their spouse until they have a business relationship with their mate. People don't know how to make friends at work, so they exist alone in a world of other people. People don't know how to make friends with their neighbors or people in their communities, so again they exist isolated and disconnected with people who are potential friends.

It is extremely helpful when a church offers classes that teach the basic skills that are required to make more friends and have deeper friendships. Sometimes these skills can be offered as one course, or they can be broken up into their basic component pieces and put into other courses or ministries. So many people feel alone or isolated in the world, and the church has the answers on how to develop people skills and lasting connections with people. We need to teach and train people in the essential actions that will allow them to create lasting friendships. People need to grow in listening skills, in understanding the required ingredients for the type of friendship they are wanting to have with the other person, and finally everyone must understand that friendships can settle out at various levels.

6. **Felt-Need Groups — solution oriented to various problems, money, parenting, marriage, etc.**
Friendships happen when people with common interests and common problems find each other and agree to share those commonalities. Most people are deeply aware of their common needs and this drives them to seek out a church or civic organization to help them. Most people also hope that there will be people just like them at this organization who can relate to what they are going through and/or go through it with them. This is why churches can and should hold Parenting classes, Marriage Improvement classes, Biblical Principles of Finance and Money, Divorce Recovery, Addiction Recovery groups, and other classes and groups that address specific problems of the community.

The church must realize that the point of the class is not just to deliver content or training. The class must also be designed to give the highest possibilities for friends. People need time to talk and interact before, during, and after the class. The more that these people connections can be facilitated, the greater sticking power the church has in its visitor retention.

I know a number of pastors who are so excited about the biblical content of the classes their church teaches that they do not design the class for any friendship building exercises or friendship time. This always causes people to leave filled up with new ideas and then trying to communicate these ideas to those who did not come to the class. Often these kinds of churches remain cold and aloof with people cycling through the various classes but not really connecting with the church in terms of commitment, service, and loyalty. A person must have deeper friendships to build a lasting loyalty to the church.

Remember, this can be aided in every class by having a small enough class for one circle to be formed instead of rows. Every person should have a nametag so that people can remember their name. Questions should be asked of the participants so that they can reveal who they are to the others in the group. Exercises and participation should be built right into the group time. Having similar kinds of people at a group or class is also helpful in building a richer friendship.

7. Life-Stage Groups — needs, interests, causes

All churches except churches with under forty should have the people divided into life-stages. The larger the church, the more narrow the life-stage definition. Whatever life stage we personally occupy is the way we see the world at that moment for the most part. Those who are teens see the world through the problems, needs, interests, and joys of a teenager. This is why most churches group young people into a youth group and do things that address the particular issues of that life-stage. The same is true for adults. There are various typical life-stages for adults and there are problems, needs, interests, and joys associated with that life-stage. Larger churches have been successful at recognizing those life-stages and developing programming, information, and training to help people with the unique challenges of that life-stage.

Developing specific life-stage groups and/or classes that address the needs, interests, and causes of a particular life-stage is very strategic. People want to hang out with people like them. For instance, if you have young pre-school children, then your parenting issues are similar to other preschool parents; you might enjoy a class or group that deals with just parenting preschoolers. Another example might be empty nesters that have more time for travel or causes than those who are still raising a family. They may enjoy being directed toward particular travel opportunities in the area or even in the state. People who have children and who are thinking about college might find a great interest in a short gathering of like-minded parents. Those who are entering retirement might enjoy getting together for breakfast meetings because of the change in their schedules. All of these are opportunities to offer friendships to people who come to the church. The gift of a deep and lasting friend should not be overlooked. We all need these loyal friends who will help us fill out our lives.

8. Common Interest/Activity Groups—sports, crafts, hobbies, activities

A final aspect of a strong friendship strategy is to build a number of groups or classes around people's common interests or activities. Churches in the past have shied away from this type of group because it did not have a clear sacred or religious purpose. This objection is being overlooked and overcome by many churches. The biblical purpose of fellowship has caused many churches to actually plan groups that have this as their main purpose to connect people as friends and Christians. More and more churches have begun using sermon-based small groups, which lends itself to being used in all kinds of contexts, including sports, crafts, hobbies, and activities. A short segment of the meeting can be devoted to the discussion of the sermon and questions. Some groups even do it during the activity where this would work.

What many churches are realizing is that people do not want another meeting to attend, but they do enjoy any excuse to do something they like doing. If that enjoyable activity or pursuit can be coupled with a spiritual discussion, then this is so much the better. This also allows the church to be a helper in the pursuit for friends who share common interests. This development of common interest groups is a good and well-balanced addition to the work of the church. In order to have a well-balanced life, one needs to have hobbies, friends, and spirituality, as well a number of other things. When these do not compete with one another, but rather enhance one another, then everybody wins.

Think through this as a visitor would. They come and see that your church has a softball team or a model railroading club or a golfing group that they can join. This says to the visitor that there are people in this church just like them. When the small group has some tie back to the sermon or to devotion to Christ, then this reconnects their spiritual commitments with their friendships.

The church must make sure that these groups regularly stop, take a few weeks off, and then start new so that people feel as though they can join and not be oddly out of place because they are the new person.

What will your church do to help people make friends?

	Needed	Cost	Time	Approval	Person
Dessert Gathering					
Small Gestures of Inclusion					
Church Orientation Program					
New Groups (Starting Constantly)					
Friendship Training					

FRIENDSHIP STRATEGY

	Needed	Cost	Time	Approval	Person
Felt-Need Groups					
Life-Stage Groups					
Common Interest Groups					
Smaller Groups					
Informal setting					
Questions					
Personal Sharing					
Nametags					
Work With, Talk With, Play With					

Conclusion

This book has focused on what your church can do to draw in more visitors and retain them. If your church will investigate the various ideas and programs that are outlined in this book, it will result in your church retaining a whole new level of those who visit your church. Remember that your church only needs to develop four key pieces in order to have an effective Assimilation Strategy. Each church is different and will need to do different things as a part of their Community Awareness Strategy, First Visit Strategy, First Weeks Strategy, and First Year Strategy. The ideas are there for any church to mix and match what will work for them in their local area and size.

I am confident that the assimilation strategies talked about in this book will work for your church. The point of this book is to build a more openly accepting and loving church so that more people can find the Savior. Your church can be a safe haven in a world full of hostility and selfishness. Most churches that I work with do not have any idea how they have become unfriendly to visitors. Many churches are stuck exactly where they are, because the people in the churches are friendly to the people that they know and tend to ignore the people they do not know. This natural strategy does not allow new people to be loved for

Christ. It does take work to do this strategy and at times it may seem overwhelming or not worth the trouble, but it is worth it to see more people identify with Christ and His church.

How many visitors would your church retain if you did all or a significant part of the above things to be welcoming and inclusive to visitors? Probably more than are being included right now. Please do not read this book and then not add anything to your Visitor Assimilation System. Add at least three things that you think would make a difference even though they may seem small or they may be a little difficult to get accomplished. A new visitor to the church is worth it.

Jesus has commissioned us to only two Great Commandments: "You shall love the Lord your God with all your heart, soul, mind, and strength and your neighbor as yourself." This assimilation plan is a way to love people. It meets their needs, it pursues them gently, and it seeks to please them so that they will come to understand the love that Christ has for them. I hope that you will agree that most churches need to be much more strategic about the way they love visitors. It is my hope that this book has filled your mind with ideas for how to help people come to find Christ and a loving fellowship in your church.

Case Study

Twin Lakes Community Church

How We Used the Four Key Strategies to Increase Visitor Assimilation to 82%

Community Awareness Strategy
First Visit Strategy

I am often asked which of the above techniques and strategies did we (TLCC) actually used to increase the visitor assimilation to 82%. The following is what we actually did:

We provided personal invitations for our members to hand out four times per year. We sent flyers out to most of the houses in our town once every few months. We put up billboards around our town that reminded people about our church. We held a number of special events every year, aimed at different age groups. We made sure that the teaching on Sunday morning was aimed at Christianity 101 or 201 levels of expertise, with one point aimed at a 401 level of depth. We had people go out to the cars a few times every Sunday morning to greet people as they walked back in. We had huge signs made so that people could see from the parking lot what each building was used for. We had four visitor's spots in the prime location in the parking lot with large signs announcing that these spots were for visitors. We stationed cheerful men and women near the front door to greet people as they came to church. We had young people ready to escort people back to the other parts of the campus to show them where the children's ministry and teen ministries took place. We had an information table with doughnuts on it and bright people standing or sitting behind it to answer questions. We had a lobby with lots of brochures and bright pictures that people could see when they stepped in the building. Lots of information was available, and there were lots of pictures of people everywhere enjoying the various ministries. We had ushers who were trained to smile and extend the bulletin to people entering the church. The ushers would direct people to the seats that were available.

We had warm and encouraging children's and teen ministry directors floating through the hallways greeting people and answering questions. We had hosts and hostesses in various sections of the congregation to greet people before the service started and to give the visitor a gift after orienting them to the upcoming service. We had opportunities in the service to recognize visitors and hand them a gift. We encouraged folks to invite a visitor out to lunch. We had people assigned each Sunday who would invite people to join them for lunch if no one else invited them. We stationed tables with doughnuts and friendly people near the exits of the church building to give people the opportunity to talk if they wanted. We thanked people for visiting the church as they left.

First Weeks Strategy and First Year Strategy

After the first visit, we then sent a couple of people to stop by the visitor's house and give them another gift as a thank you for visiting our church. Early Sunday evening the senior pastor would call the visitors and thank them for calling and see if they had any questions. On Tuesday we would send out a welcome letter from the church thanking them for visiting the church and telling them about many of the programs at the church that were designed to serve them.

We assumed that they would come the very next Sunday. We then had a staff person phone them after the second Sunday. We then sent them a brochure about the ministry that they would seem to be the most interested in based upon the staff phone call. We then began to invite them to the Newcomer's Dessert at the pastor's home.

We also would send cards and phone the visitor to invite them to the new church orientation classes that were starting. Each separate class was an opportunity to invite them to attend and meet new people and learn new things about the church. We started new small groups every eight weeks and invited everyone who was attending the church to be a part of these new groups. There were usually eight to ten new groups starting every eight weeks.

We worked hard to include new people in serving opportunities by calling them to ask if they would like to be involved in various ministries. We offered training classes and one-on-one training for people to learn a particular job that needed volunteers around the church. We had various events and groups getting together around different interests and ideas so that people would be able to meet the largest number of people with whom they might be able to connect.

You can see that our church did not do all of the things in this book because we were only a middle-size church of between five hundred and seven hundred.

As we grew, we kept adding in the various elements of a larger assimilation plan. This is the same way that you will build your assimilation plan. You will add a few things to improve the way you are welcoming visitors now, and a few more and a few more as God gives you just the right mix and you are retaining a high number of those who come to your church.

Take a look at this list of activities that our church did and put a check in the box to the right if you believe that you should do this activity.

CASE STUDY

Assimilation Strategy (_____) Church	Will We Do This?
Flyers out to most of the houses in our town once every few months.	
Billboards around our town that remind people about our church.	
Special events every year aimed at different ages.	
Teaching on Sunday morning aimed at Christianity 101 or 201 levels of expertise with one point aimed at a 401 level of depth.	
People going out to the cars a few times every Sunday morning and greeting people as they walk back in.	
Huge signs made so that people can see from the parking lot what a building is used for.	
_____# of visitor spots right in the prime location in the parking lot with large signs announcing these spots are for visitors.	
Cheerful men and women stationed near the front door to greet people as they come to church.	
Young people ready to escort people back to the other parts of the campus to show the people where the children's ministry and teen ministries take place.	
An information table with doughnuts and bright people standing or sitting behind it to answer questions.	
A lobby with lots of brochures and bright pictures that people can see when they step in the building.	

Assimilation Strategy (_____) Church	Will We Do This?
Lots of information is available and lots of pictures of people are everywhere showing them enjoying the various ministries.	
Ushers trained to smile and extend the bulletin to people entering the church.	
Ushers direct people to the seats that are available.	
Warm and encouraging children's and teen ministry directors float through the hallways, greeting people and answering questions.	
Hosts and hostesses in various sections of the congregation to greet people before the service starts and to give the visitor a gift after orienting them to the upcoming service.	
Opportunities in the service to recognize visitors and hand them a gift.	
Encouraging folks to invite a visitor out to lunch.	
People assigned each Sunday who will invite people to join them for lunch if no one else invites them.	
Tables with doughnuts and friendly people near the exits of the church building to give people the opportunity to talk if they want to.	
Thanking people for visiting the church as they leave.	
People stop by a visitor's house and give them another gift as a thank you for visiting our church.	

CASE STUDY

Assimilation Strategy (_____) Church	Will We Do This?
Senior Pastor calls the visitors and thanks them for coming and checks to see if they have any questions.	
Tuesday, a welcome letter goes out from the church thanking them for visiting the church and telling them about many of the programs at the church that are designed to serve them.	
Assume that they will come the very next Sunday.	
Staff person phones them after the second Sunday.	
Send a brochure about the ministry based upon the staff phone call.	
Invite visitors to the Newcomer's Dessert at the pastor's home.	
Send cards and phone the visitor to invite them to the new church orientation classes that are starting.	
Each class is an opportunity to invite and meet new people and learn new things about the church.	
Starting new small groups every eight weeks and inviting everyone attending the church to be a part of these new groups. There are usually eight to ten new groups starting every eight weeks.	
Include new people in serving opportunities by calling them to ask if they would like to be involved in various ministries.	
Offering training classes and one-on-one training for people to learn a particular job that needs volunteers around the church.	

Assimilation Strategy (_____) Church	Will We Do This?
Various events and groups get together around different interests and ideas so that people can meet the largest number of people with whom they might be able to connect.	

Your church may want to build a table like the one above and say what you are doing and what you need to do so that you can reach the people that God is already sending you.

We strived to be what Jesus called us to be: lovers of people and fishers of men. We were collecting those people whom Jesus loves into communities of faith so that they more perfectly can learn to love Him and others.

As God sends your church a steady stream of visitors, I pray that you will be able to capture more than your share and that your church will break open with all the people who want to be a part of your community of faith.

How to Use this Book Most Effectively

The best way to take the most advantage of this material is to get a group together to evaluate it and make a practical list of what could be added to your church to make it more effective at assimilation. The group should also discuss the ways to implement the ideas in your church. Appoint a captain of Assimilation as the person who will champion this crucial ministry towards health. The captain does not have to be the leader of the Assimilation Ministry, but they need to make sure that the assimilation of new people does not settle back into something that the church hopes takes place. A captain of Assimilation ensures that a person other than the pastor is commissioned with a focus on keeping visitors coming back until they are fully functioning members of the church.

Have the group make recommendations to the pastor and the board on two to three changes that could be made to each of the four key assimilation strategies in your church. Do not try and do it all. You will try some things that will work, and you will try some things that will not work in your local context. It is okay. Not everything that is mentioned in this book will work where you are doing ministry. But be actively improving.

"FOLLOW ME,"
Jesus said, "and I will make you Fishers of Men."
MATTHEW 4:19

About the Author

Dr. Gil Stieglitz is an author, speaker, catalyst, professor, and leadership consultant. He currently serves as Discipleship Pastor at Bayside Church, a dynamic multi-site church on the Northside of Sacramento, CA. He served for five years as Executive Pastor of Adventure Christian Church in Roseville, California. He is an adjunct professor at Western Seminary (Sacramento Campus), a church consultant for Thriving Churches International, and Founder and President of Principles to Live By, a non-profit discipleship and publishing organization. He is on the board at Courage Worldwide, a wonderful organization that rescues children forced into sexual slavery. He has been a denominational executive for thirteen years with the Evangelical Church of America. He was the senior pastor at a mid-sized church in Southern California for seventeen years.

To learn more about Gil, his books, resources, and teaching and consulting opportunities, visit www.ptlb.com.

Other Resources by Gil Stieglitz

BOOKS
Becoming a Godly Husband
Becoming Courageous
Breakfast with Solomon, Volumes 1 - 3
Breaking Satanic Bondage
Deep Happiness: The Eight Secrets
Delighting in God
Delighting in Jesus
Developing a Christian Worldview
God's Radical Plan for Wives
Going Deep In Prayer: Forty Days of In-Depth Prayer
Leading a Thriving Ministry
Marital Intelligence
Mission Possible: Winning the Battle Over Temptation
Proverbs: A Devotional Commentary, Volumes 1 - 2
Satan and The Origin of Evil
Secrets of God's Armor
Spiritual Disciplines of a C.H.R.I.S.T.I.A.N
The Schemes of Satan
They Laughed When I Wrote Another Book About Prayer, Then They Read It
Touching the Face of God: Forty Days of Adoring God
Weapons of Righteousness Study Guides
Why There Has to Be a Hell

OTHER RESOURCES

PODCASTS

Becoming a Godly Parent

Biblical Meditation: The Keys of Transformation

Deep Happiness: The Eight Secrets

Everyday Spiritual Warfare Series

God's Guide to Handling Money

Marital Intelligence: There are Only Five Problems in Marriage

Intensive Spiritual Warfare Series

Spiritual War Surrounding Money

The Four Keys to a Great Family

The Ten Commandments

Thrive Conference:

- Marital Intelligence: There are Only Five Problems in Marriage
- Raising Your Leadership Level: Double Your Impact
- Spiritual Warfare: Using the Weapons of God to Win Spiritual Battles

Weapons of Righteousness Series

If you would be interested in having Gil Stieglitz speak to your group, you can contact him through the website
www.ptlb.com

www.ingramcontent.com/pod-product-compliance
Lightning Source LLC
Chambersburg PA
CBHW060524100426
42743CB00009B/1425